TO *CATCH* _____
_____ A DREAM

SUNY Series in Dream Studies
Robert L. Van de Castle, Editor

TO *CATCH* _____
_____ A DREAM

Explorations of Dreaming

DAVID KOULACK

State University of New York Press

21151063

BF
1078
·K68
1991

Published by
State University of New York Press, Albany

For information, address State University of New York Press,
State University Plaza, Albany, N.Y., 12246

Library of Congress Cataloging-in-Publication Data

Koulack, David.
　　To catch a dream : explorations of dreaming / David Koulack.
　　　　p. cm.—(SUNY series in dream studies)
　　Includes bibliographical references.
　　ISBN 0-7914-0501-X—ISBN 0-7914-0502-8 (pbk.)
　　1. Dreams.　　I. Title.　　II. Series.
　　BF1078.K68　　1991
　　154.6′3—dc20　　　　　　　　　　　　　　　　　　90-31667
　　　　　　　　　　　　　　　　　　　　　　　　　　　　　　CIP

10　9　8　7　6　5　4　3　2

In memory of my father

CONTENTS

Contents

PREFACE

Dreaming. Its mysteries have captured the imagination of playwrights and poets, courtiers and kings. Its products provide all of us with glimpses of our creative abilities at their best. But what purpose if any does dreaming serve?

In this book I've tried to provide some tentative answers to this intriguing question. But there were other things I wanted to do as well. For those who've never had the opportunity to experience the excitement and frustrations of dream research, I've endeavored to convey a picture of what this strange activity is all about. For my colleagues, I've tried to provide a chronicle of their valiant efforts as they have attempted to unlock the secrets of dreaming. Along the way I've tried to place the interest in and research on dreams and dreaming into an historical perspective.

I wouldn't have had an opportunity to write this book if it hadn't been for a number of people who helped me along the way. A long time ago Dick Held, Ulric Neisser and Jim Klee had confidence in me when I had none in myself. Richard Jones' enthusiasm about dreams piqued my own curiosity. Irv Rock, Morris Eagle and Arthur Shapiro gave me encouragement and support. Herman Witkin gave me my first opportunity to do dream research. And finally, there were Don Goodenough and Joseph De Koninck—one a teacher, the other a student—colleagues and dear friends from whom I learned more than I can say.

ACKNOWLEDGMENTS

I gratefully acknowledge the permission granted by the following publishers and copyright owners to reprint selections from their publications:

Rosette for her dream and analyses.

Garland Publishing, Inc. for J. Gackenbach (Ed.) *Sleep and Dreams: A Sourcebook.*

Charles C. Thomas for M. Kramer (Ed.) *Dream Psychology and the New Biology of Dreaming.*

Random House for H. A. Witkin and H. B. Lewis, (Eds.) *Experimental Studies of Dreaming.*

1

Sleeping and Dreaming

ROSETTE'S DREAM

The jungle is dark and lusciously green. The river is deep and narrow, a brilliant blue. It is night but the sky is also a luminous deep blue with the light of the moon shining on the tropical forest and the flesh of the naked woman standing in the turbulent river. The water swirls around her thighs as she reaches deep for the iridescent fish that swim and dart all around her. They are large and strong and slip between her arms as she tries to catch them with her bare hands. I know as I dream that she is my mother. I have a feeling of beauty and strength but of something ominous and sinister as well. At last she manages to grasp the tail of a great squirming fish, its scales glinting and eyes staring as she throws it over her shoulder with both arms. She turns away to walk determinedly upstream through the river towards the distant horizon where the sun is rising. In that same instant, the living fish slung across her broad back becomes a dead fish and its silvery skin and pink flesh dissolve to reveal a bony white skeleton. The woman feels the weight of the bones but she

pushes her way through the water with power
and concentration. I can't be sure whether I am
having a good or a bad dream but I know I will
not forget it. Like a cut in film the scene
changes:

The hot sun burns in the pale yellow sky as I am
attempting my first solo flight in a tiny airplane,
flying over a grey sea that is bordered by my
mother's jungle. I am very afraid and my heart is
pounding. I just make a landing on a small sand
bar in the shallow sea, miles away from the
shore. It is difficult but I make the landing. I feel
exhilarated and very proud.

When I awoke the dream was intensely present
in my mind and I was utterly certain of its central
importance to me. It has remained precise and
clear and just as intensely vivid ever since. I had
this dream two years ago.

It was one Saturday evening that Rosette told me her
dream. We were sitting down to dinner at the home of a
mutual friend. Rosette, on hearing that I was involved in
dream research, insisted on relating her dream to me.

A hush came over the table as she began to speak.
Rosette not only described her dream but also related her
associations to it and her understanding of it. Later, I
asked her to write it all down for me.

ROSETTE'S FIRST ANALYSIS

I spoke to a therapist about the dream but could
make very little sense of the images although I
appreciated the overall significance of the "solo
flight." At the time, I was newly separated from
my husband, an Italian archeologist working for
long periods of time in Crete. I expected to

understand something about myself and believed the naked woman must be an inner pro-
jection of myself and not my mother at all. I looked
into the Jungian and Freudian literature and
found that fish dreams were to be interpreted as
memories of birth. I tried to make a connection
between my dream and the birth of my children
but could find no satisfactory explanation,
nothing that unlocked the images in a meaningful way. I knew that I had to "solve" the
dream: it presented itself as a sign for something
else that I needed to know. I told my dream to
many friends hoping to find some explanation or
insight, but found none.

THE STORY OF ROSETTE'S MOTHER

More than a year later, my mother came to visit
me in Leicester where I had a teaching post. She
came to Europe most summers and always
spent some of her holiday each year with a
friend in London, a woman with whom she had
survived from a Nazi concentration camp. I
knew very little about her experiences and she
never initiated any conversation on that subject.
But on the second day of her visit she came into
the kitchen and said she had something important to tell me. I had my back to her as I was
washing the lunch dishes but I listened as she
told me very calmly if briefly that before the war
she had been married to an older man and had
had a child, a daughter who had died in the
camp. I was overcome with sorrow and burst
into tears, something which only very rarely happens to me. She cried a little too and I remember
putting my arms around her with my dripping
rubber gloves still on. I asked a few questions
and learned the father of the child was still alive.

He and my mother had been hiding with members of his family when they had been arrested and sent to the concentration camp. When they arrived, the father understood a selection was being made and that women with young children were being put in a separate group. He took the child from my mother's arms and gave her to his sister to hold. His sister and her own two children as well as my mother's seventeen-month-old baby were taken away and never seen again. My mother would tell me little else but the following summer she gave me two snapshots of herself and her sister-in-law with their babies. She said nothing but that I should look after the photos as they were "history."

ROSETTE'S ANSWER

My mother's revelation to me of her loss had a momentous effect on me. At the same instant I felt grief, and a communion of feeling as a mother myself, I was filled with an awareness of a lightening sensation in the top of my head. I felt enormous relief and the thought crossed my mind that at last I would no longer have to be everything that the lost child might have been. I was simultaneously surprised to be thinking such a thing and also angry and confused that I had not been told earlier, at least twenty years earlier. As I stood there with my mother wondering how her forty-year-old secret had suddenly taken her away from me and also brought me closer, the images of my dream flashed through my mind and I felt something inside my mind fall into place with a satisfying certainty. Unconsciously I had created an image of my mother courageously carrying the burden of her dead child through her troubled life, while I tried to meet the challenge of navigating in a near empty sea. So much of her energy had always been directed toward keeping her pain at bay. I have been coming to terms with the ghost of my half sister ever since my mother told me her story, but I also know that somehow I always knew, If not the facts, at least the effects of that child's murder. I believe my dream was the materialization of all the felt emotions and pressures, a very rational conclusion that my brain had come to from a mass of information about my relationship with my mother. My dream was an intuition: a knowledge without conscious thought.

Rosette's dream is of course unique to her, as is her interpretation of it and her associations to it. However, what isn't special is her fascination with it. She found her dream to be intriguing. It seemed to her that her dream was somehow related to events in her life that actually predated her existence.

Rosette's interest in and speculation about the meaning of her dream mirrors the concerns with dreams expressed through the ages in many different societies. Their mysterious, surrealistic quality and the glimpses of a strange and unknown world they provide have caused people to wonder about their meaning and speculate on their potential prophetic properties.

EARLY THOUGHTS ON SLEEP AND DREAMS

The earliest evidence we have of interest in dreams is ancient Egyptian dream books written about 2000 B.C. They're essentially books of dream interpretation, listing types of dreams people may have and what each of them may mean for the future of the dreamer. The Old and New Testaments also are replete with accounts of prophetic dreams and the work of skilled dream interpreters. One of the most famous of these interpreters, of course, was Joseph.

Joseph was brought to the attention of the Pharaoh by the chief Butler who had been in jail with Joseph. While there, the chief Butler and the Baker each had dreams. The Butler's dream was of a vine with three branches from which he took grapes to press into the cup of the Pharaoh. The Baker dreamed of carrying three baskets on his head from which the birds ate. On the basis of the dreams Joseph accurately predicted the return to favor of the Butler and the imminent demise of the Baker. The rest, as they say, is history.

Other individuals, not so concerned with the prophetic qualities of dreams, were struck by their apparent aid to the creative process. Robert Louis Stevenson, for example, would have claimed that as a creative aid, dreams have no peer. He noted that many of his stories were in reality transcriptions, with some changes or embellishments, of dreams he himself had had. But perhaps one of the most famous of stories concerning dreams and the creative process is that of Fredrich Kekulé, a professor of organic chemistry at Ghent University around the middle of the nineteenth century. Trying to solve the mystery of the atom configuration of the benzine molecule, Kekulé went to bed one night with the problem very much on his mind. During the night, he dreamed of a snake with its tail in its mouth. On awakening, he interpreted the dream as signifying the closed ring of the benzine molecule and the mystery was solved.

Admittedly, we aren't all Kekulés or Stevensons or Rosettes, for that matter, but we do have something very much in common with them. We are all dreamers. Many of us have at one time or another marveled at our own dreams and wondered at their meaning. Some of us, no doubt, have gained insight from our dreams, others may well have found them an aid in solving problems, and still others may have found them a stimulus to creativity. But all of us who remember our dreams now and then have certainly been struck on one occasion or another by their vividness and their compelling quality.

Dreams, oddly enough, are at once a shared and unique experience. They are shared because we all have them. They are unique because they are peculiar to each one of us. They seem to both reflect and respond to our own personal experience. Consequently it's really not surprising that down through history people have marveled at and tried to unravel the mystery of dreams.

The puzzle is perhaps made even more enticing because dreams by definition are embedded in sleep, itself a mysterious state currently undergoing vigorous investigation. At one time, sleep was thought to be a passive rather than an active process.[1] That is, sleep was considered to be merely a cessation of wakefulness. With the discovery of centers of the brain responsible for sleep, the pendulum has swung in the direction of the belief that sleep is actively induced by these centers. Nevertheless, one of the biggest questions that still remains is why we sleep at all!

Similar debates had been ongoing as to why we dream.[2] Philosophers from the time of Aristotle into the twentieth century presented arguments for and against dreaming as an active, self-induced process. On one hand, there was a school of thought that suggested that dreams were somehow produced by external stimulation. On the other hand, there were those who thought that dreams were ultimately products of the individual's mind. This latter view essentially suggested a continuity in functioning between the waking and sleeping states. But here again, just as with sleep, the question of great moment remains: Why do we dream?

COMMON NOTIONS ABOUT SLEEP AND DREAMS

Probably because we're all active participants in the sleeping and dreaming business, each of us has our own pet theory about the function of sleep and dreams.

For example, some think we sleep to restore our bodies from the physical demands of waking life. It's almost as if we run down like a clock and sleep is the mechanism by which we get wound up again. Along with this view goes the notion that we need a certain amount of sleep each night (usually thought to be eight hours) in order to function properly the next day. Still others think we sleep to dream, that dreaming is essential for proper functioning while awake, and sleep simply provides the medium for this activity. I'll have occasion to talk about these ideas a bit more when we examine some of the research on sleep and dream deprivation.

Common notions about dreaming are far greater in number than those about sleep, perhaps because as I mentioned before, dreams are often such riveting events they apparently seem to have to be there for a reason. Some of the earliest ideas about dreaming which I've already described have found their way into the twentieth century virtually unaltered.

There are people, for example, who believe that dreams foretell the future. In fact it's surprising to me how many people have called me up over the years dismayed because they were certain their dreams were predictive in nature. The dismay usually resulted because a dream of theirs had depicted an impending disaster occurring to themselves or to someone they knew. On careful probing, it invariably turned out that in past years these people had had a dream or two that they were able to vaguely inter-pret as premonitions that were ultimately fulfilled. The fact that such premonitions could have been coincidences much like those that occasionally take place during the waking state, never occurred to them. Also, the fact that the vast majority of their dreams had nothing to do with the accurate prediction of future events was readily dis-counted. Rather, it was the striking, catastrophic quality of their recent dream coupled with a seemingly predictive dream in the past that made them certain their dreams were ultimately portents of the future.

Another common notion is that dreams emanate from the experiences of the previous day or even those of the distant past. No doubt, the appearance in our dreams of events and conversations we've actually experienced as well as places and people we know provide compelling evidence for this speculation. Not unrelated to this notion is the idea that dreams somehow serve a problem-solving function. Some think that people going to bed with a problem on their mind (like Kekulé) continue to work toward a solution which may be revealed to them in their dreams.

Another idea, similar to the one espoused by Rosette, is that dreams arise from unconscious experiences. In her situation, Rosette felt that somehow she had known of her mother's terrible loss without being consciously aware of it. For Rosette, the dream reflected this awareness and brought it into consciousness.

And finally, of course, there is what Hadfield[3] called the "Heavy Supper Theory," the idea that dreams are caused by indigestion or other bodily disturbances. Hadfield suggested there is a certain credibility to this theory: "A heavy supper, by drawing blood for the digestion, may affect the circulation of the brain and so give rise to the dream" (p. 5). However, he went on to point out it doesn't account for what we dream. "Four men have a supper of pork and beans, but whereas one may dream of his lady-love, another dreams of being pursued by horrible monsters, another of being murdered, another of a failing business" (p. 5).

So there in a nutshell Hadfield placed his finger on the two central and related issues I alluded to before. Why do we dream? That is, what causes us to dream? And what determines the actual content of our dreams? Most early and common dream notions seemed to confuse the two issues and treat them as one. In the twentieth century, the perpetuation of this confusion may in large part be due to the influence of Sigmund Freud.[4] His monumental work, *The Interpretation of Dreams*, not only de-emphasized concerns with the physiology of sleep[5] but also thrust to the forefront of theory and investigation the notion that dreams are products of various forms of stimulation. In doing so, Freud ignored the possibility that dreaming may be a self-generated product of the brain and a sleeping analogue of waking thought. We'll have occasion to examine this possibility later on.

We'll also take a more careful look at some of the ideas of Freud. In the final analysis, in whatever way we end up assessing his work, Freud's impact on contemporary theory and research on dreams probably cannot be overestimated. But before getting into all of this, I think it's important to get a feel for some of the difficulties involved in doing dream research. I know of no other field in psychology as fraught with obstacles as this peculiar area of investigation.

RESEARCH ON DREAMS

Probably the main difficulty in dream research, even with modern day techniques, is that we are always dealing with memories of past events. As Norman Malcolm[6] pointed out, the sentence "I am dreaming" is essentially meaningless in reference to events taking place during sleep. It is only on waking that we can say, "I was dreaming." Consequently, reports of dreaming are subject to the vagaries of our memories.

Telling someone about our dreams is not unlike trying to tell friends about a movie or television show we have seen recently. Generally, we don't provide them with a detailed, blow by blow account. We tell them of some striking events which happened to stick in our memories. And we might provide them with a theme or thread of some sort to hold those events together. Similarly, when we describe our dreams on waking, we are likely to describe only incidents or events that have particular significance to us. However, unlike a description of a movie or television show, the description of the dream is solely the property of the dreamer. There is no way for our friends to go back and examine what it is we are talking about as they could in the case of a publicly available event. So in the end, all that a dream researcher has to work with is the *report* of the memory of the dream, not the dream itself.

And memory, particularly when it involves recall of dreams, is more fragile than most of us realize. I'll talk more about this later when we discuss dream recall and dream recall failure, but suffice it to say for the moment that recall in general is not a simple process. And in the case of dreams it may be hampered by sleep itself.

As if this were not problem enough, in relating the dream to another person, the dreamer is often trying to translate a primarily visual, sometimes emotional, often disjointed experience into a form intelligible to the listener. Rosette's dream and subsequent report is a wonderful example of the process. Her dream was filled with exquisite visual images and profound emotions. Rosette managed to translate those images and feelings into words. But there are questions that still remain. How good a job did she do? How much has she left out? How much has she added? We'll probably never be able to have definitive answers to these questions. However, we can be certain that some degree of distortion has taken place.

In the telling of the dream, the dreamer is likely to fill in details to make the dream more comprehensible both to him or herself and to the listener. The dreamer must fit the memory of the dream into the grammar of a language. There is a little experiment by Bartlett[7] that neatly illustrates the implications of this process. He gave a translation of a North American Indian folk tale to people in England to read. The story had a number of vivid images and in some cases the incidents had no obvious interconnection. After reading the story, the subjects were asked to reproduce it. Bartlett found that in general the story was shortened, was presented in what he termed a journalistic style and was placed in a framework more coherent than that of the original.

Presumably a similar sort of process goes on in dream reporting. The dreamer is often trying to convey an unconnected series of images to the dream researcher. The researcher in turn must try to understand the dream from the perspective of the dreamer. Even with the best of intentions on the part of the dreamer and the most careful, objective inquiry on the part of the researcher, all that finally remains is a product which is an unverifiable, probably somewhat distorted version of a very personal experience.

What this means, finally, is that those of us involved in dream research have had to go at our subject in a rather roundabout manner. We have had to peck away at an elusive event. And we have had to try to understand the source and function of that event on the basis of some very fragile data—the report of the memory of dreams. In spite of those difficulties, some exciting and interesting inroads have been made into the world of dreams.

2

Freud and Dreaming

As we noted earlier, Freud's work, and in particular *The Interpretation of Dreams* had a profound impact on attempts to understand the function of dreams. The threads of his influence can be found running through the notions of many theorists who followed him. They can also be found in the nature of the interpretations we often apply to our own dreams.

Take Rosette's dream (chapter 1) for example. In her first attempt to "solve" the dream, Rosette looked to the work of Freud (and Jung) to unlock the images in a meaningful way. It's not fish, but it is water which Freud described as signifying birth. "A large number of dreams, often accompanied by anxiety and having as their content such subjects as passing through narrow spaces or being in water, are based upon phantasies of intra-uterine life, of existence in the womb and of the act of birth."[1] Rosette tried to make the connection between the dream and the birth of her own children but remained dissatisfied. It was only after her mother revealed to Rosette the birth and death of Rosette's half sister that she was able to understand her dream as a materialization of all the felt emotions and pressures surrounding the child's murder.

Okay, we'll buy that interpretation. So what's the function of dreams in general and Rosette's dream in par-

ticular? To put it another way, do dreams have any purpose or utility? This is not a simple question because it's
not always clear what we mean by the term "function"
when we apply it to dreams. There is often a confusion
between the function dreams may have in a therapeutic
setting and the role they may play in maintaining our
well-being in general. Part of the quandary probably
results from common misconceptions about Freud and
his notions, misconceptions perpetuated to some extent
by Freud himself.[2] And part of the confusion might come
from the very nature of dreams themselves.

To better understand this problem and what is meant
by the term "function" as applied to dreams, it's worth
considering the distinction Jones[3] made between dream
interpretation and dream investigation.

EXPLORING DREAMS

There are two related yet divergent pathways for exploring dreams. Jones referred to them as dream interpretation and dream investigation. He characterized
dream interpretation as a social event. Why? Because it
often involves the exchange of exquisite, personal detail
between individuals and by implication brings with it a
certain emotional intimacy and trust. According to Jones,
the goal of dream interpretation is to enhance the quality
of an individual's waking life. And as he suggested dream
interpretation derives its validity from its consistency
with other information about the life of the dreamer.

Rosette's quest for an understanding of her dream
and her final analysis of it is a good example of what Jones
is talking about. She told her dream to a therapist and "to
many friends hoping to find explanation or insight." When
Rosette finally solved the mystery of her dream her
descriptions of her feelings are almost palpable: "the images of my dream flashed through my mind and I felt
something in my mind fall into place with a satisfying certainty." And of course, the dream interpretation derived

its validity from its consistency with the newly discovered information Rosette had about her life: "My dream was an intuition: a knowledge without conscious thought."

Dream investigation, on the other hand, need not be a social event. Dreams of people we don't know can be collected and fruitfully examined apart from the dreamer in order to better understand the psychological processes underlying dreaming. The goal of dream investigation is to understand the state of dreaming itself rather than to enhance the quality of waking life. The validity of such an investigation is measured not by the dreamer's response but by scientific criteria. For example, can the findings be replicated at different times and in different laboratories? Are new findings logically consistent with facts already existing in the arena of information about dreams? And so forth.

Taken within the context of this dichotomy between dream interpretation and dream investigation, the meaning of the word function as it applies to dreams can be understood in two entirely different ways. In the former case, the dream, or rather the memory of the dream, is used in the waking state to help reveal something about the dreamer. It is used by the dream analyst as a tool to recover or uncover information of importance to the dreamer.

In the latter case, the dream is not a tool but the object of exploration. The question of function is a question of purpose as well as a question of the mode of operation.[4] What role if any do dreams play in our lives in general and in our sleeping lives in particular?

In Jones' view, Freud, intent as he was on providing a meaningful method for intepreting dreams, did not always carefully observe the dichotomy between dream interpretation and dream investigation. Jones felt this failure has been amplified over time. As a consequence, the threads of these two modes of endeavor have tended to become more intertwined than ever before. Our job will be to untangle them as best we can. It won't be a simple task.

As we'll see in the next chapter when we explore the workings of a sleep laboratory, the boundaries drawn by Jones between dream investigation and dream interpretation are often overstepped. It's not just because of the legacy of Freud. It seems to be intrinsic to the nature of the exploration of dreaming. For example, the element of trust which figures so prominently in dream interpretation is also important in the process of dream investigation. Within the relatively sterile and certainly peculiar surroundings of the sleep laboratory, subjects place themselves in the hands of an experimenter. Trustingly, they allow themselves to be harnessed to machinery and monitored as they drift off to sleep. Still later, they willingly recount their dreams. The trust is in fact mutual. The experimenter has to have ultimate confidence the subjects will truthfully and as faithfully as possible report what was going through their minds before they were awakened.

Thus, there is a profound trust and a certain intimacy that necessarily develops between the subject and experimenter, between the dreamer and the dream researcher. To my knowledge, this degree of trust and intimacy has no equal in any other field of psychological research. Consequently, the very process of dream investigation is often washed with elements intrinsic to dream interpretation.

FREUD'S NOTIONS OF DREAM FUNCTION

Wish-Fulfillment

Wish-fulfillment would seem to be a simple term. It means literally the fulfillment of a wish. But oddly enough, Freud didn't use the term to designate the fulfillment of *a* wish. He used it as a rubric to describe at least two types of wishes occurring at the same time: unconscious impulses or wishes and the wish to sleep. He acknowledged that a third type also could occur. Freud gave the third type less importance than the other two, yet it is the third type which all of us seem to think of when we are confronted by the term wish-fulfillment.

Let's take another look at a segment of Rosette's dream for a moment. In the second scene of her dream, Rosette is attempting her "first solo flight in a tiny airplane." She is very afraid. Finally, she makes a landing on a small sand bar. She feels "exhilarated and very proud."

In her association to this segment, Rosette understood the solo flight to relate to her recent marital circumstances. She had just separated from her husband and was in reality alone for the first time. Her life situation, precipitously altered, left her with feelings of dismay and anxiety. At times Rosette wondered if she would be able to handle her new found responsibilities in a capable manner. In the dream, she similarly experienced anxiety as she made a solo flight in a tiny airplane. And in the dream, she successfully completed the journey, just as she would like to complete it in her waking life. In short, we might say the dream represented the fulfillment of Rosette's wish to make a successful go of her life.

Freud would no doubt agree with this interpretation. Take for example one of Freud's own, often cited dreams, his dream about one of his patients, Irma. In the dream Freud encountered Irma in a great hall with numerous guests. He reproached her for not accepting his "solution" to her problem. Irma looked "pale and puffy." Freud began to examine her and ultimately called in Dr. M. as well. Then his friends Otto and Leopold (both doctors) appeared as the examination continued. They discovered an infection. And finally, Freud dreamed, "We were directly aware, too, of the origin of her infection. Not long before, when she was feeling unwell, my friend Otto had given her an injection of a preparation. . . . Injections of that sort ought not to be made so thoughtlessly. . . . And probably the syringe had not been clean."[5]

As it turned out, the day before Freud had this dream, he had in fact encountered his friend Otto. Otto happened to have been staying with Freud's patient Irma at a country resort. Freud's treatment of Irma which had broken off for the summer had ended in what Freud termed "a partial success." When Freud asked Otto how Irma was, Otto replied, "She's better, but not quite well." Freud felt he could detect a note of reproof in Otto's tone, as if he was chastening Freud for promising his patient too much. That evening, Freud wrote out Irma's case history with the idea of giving it to Dr. M. to justify himself. And that night Freud had his Irma dream.

After a lengthy and detailed interpretation of the dream, Freud had this to say, "The conclusion of the dream . . . was that I was not responsible for the persistence of Irma's pains, but that Otto was. Otto had in fact annoyed me by his remarks about Irma's incomplete cure, and the dream gave me revenge by throwing the reproach back on him. The dream acquitted me of the responsibility for Irma's condition by showing that it was due to other factors. . . . The dream represented a particular state of affairs as I should have wished it to be. *Thus its content was the fulfilment of a wish and its motive was a wish.*"[6]

So what of these other types of wishes we mentioned earlier? What are they and how do they come about?

The Wish to Sleep

Here's what Freud had to say about sleep in a paper published sixteen years after *The Interpretation of Dreams*:

> "We are not accustomed to expend much thought on the fact that every night human beings lay aside their garments they pull over their skin, and even also other objects which they use to supplement their bodily organs (so far as they have succeeded in making good their deficiencies by substitutes)—for instance, their spectacles, false hair or teeth, and so on. In addition to this, when they go to sleep they perform

an analogous dismantling of their minds—they lay aside most of their mental acquisitions; thus both physically and mentally approaching remarkably close to the situation in which they began life. Somatically, sleep is an act which reproduces intrauterine existence, fulfilling the conditions of repose, warmth and the absence of stimulus; indeed in sleeping, many people resume the foetal position. The feature characterizing the mind of a sleeping person is an almost complete withdrawal from the surrounding world and the cessation of all interest in it."[7]

As Freud so aptly noted, we don't usually give very much thought to our nightly preparations for sleep. While we may engage in our own special nightly rituals as we prepare for bed we are generally almost unaware of the process of going to sleep and sleeping. Nor do we think very much, if ever, about why we sleep. In a sense, we might say, Freud was no different from anyone else. He had little to say about why we go to sleep, he just acknowledged that we do it on a regular basis. Apparently because sleep occurs with such unrelenting regularity Freud made the assumption that there is a *"wish to sleep."*[8] And even though the wish to sleep is almost an add on, catch phrase, it plays a peculiarly prominent role in Freud's notion of the function of dreams. This is because from time to time sleep is threatened by various types of intrusive events. At those times dreams serve the purpose of maintaining sleep. *"Dreams are the GUARDIANS of sleep and not its disturbers."*[9]

If dreams are the "guardians" of sleep, from what are they protecting it? What forces are threatening to waken the sleeper? And how are these forces to be thwarted? According to Freud, there are a number of forces which have the potential to disturb sleep. Among these are external stimuli such as noise and light that may waken the sleeper. There are also internal, physical stimuli such as hunger or a full bladder that can intrude on sleep. And finally, there are internal psychic stimuli. The internal psychic stimuli are unconscious impulses or wishes. They harbor the greatest danger for sleep.

We'll examine the impact external and internal physical stimuli may have on sleep and dreaming in a moment. We'll also consider Freud's view of unconscious impulses or wishes and their important role in the creation of dreams. But first let's examine the origins of those unconscious wishes and their relationship to dreaming.

Wishes and Dreaming

Essentially Freud conceived of the brain as a system responsible for discharging energy. Energy could be built up as a result of both internal and external excitation. In order to better understand this system,* and also to understand the origins of unconscious wishes, let's take a brief look at its development.

In infancy, the basic function of the system is to keep itself as free from collected energy as possible. It does this through movement. To take a simple example, if you smile and say "Coochy, coo" to a baby, and the baby smiles back or kicks its legs in response, it is discharging the energy of your stimulation (visual and auditory) by its motor activity (smiling and moving its legs).

This is all well and good until certain hard facts of life, generally in the form of internal stimulation set in. Freud used an example of a hungry baby to illustrate this point. When the baby is hungry, no amount of kicking or screaming (or general motor activity) can reduce the hunger. Unlike your playful chat with the baby, hunger is *continuous*, not momentary. The only thing that can reduce or discharge the energy created by the hunger is for someone to feed the baby. According to Freud, at this point a connection is made in the baby's brain between the particular need (in this case hunger) and the satisfaction of the need (in this case eating food).

---

*Freud called this system the "mental apparatus."

Now here comes the interesting part. The next time the baby gets hungry, there is an attempt to re-establish the source of satisfaction. That is, the brain tries to connect the stimulation of hunger with the *memory* of the food that was the original source of satisfaction. The impulse to re-establish this connection is a "wish." The reappearance of the food (in the imagination of the baby) constitutes the "fulfillment of the wish."

Of course, we all learn quite quickly that fantasizing about food doesn't do much in the way of reducing our hunger. Consequently we begin to seek satisfaction for our needs, at least in our waking lives, in the real world. We become more efficient at expending our psychic energy. Instead of using hallucinations and fantasy in seeking satisfaction, we look to sources that may very well provide it.

What has happened, according to Freud, is that we have now learned to think about and direct our movement toward *actually* obtaining satisfaction. Instead of merely imagining satisfaction we can actively and effectively seek it out. Thinking has in essence superseded an infantile way of functioning. And *"Dreaming is a piece of infantile mental life that has been superseded."*[10]

Within this framework, Freud's analogy of dreaming to infantile mental life becomes quite clear. While we sleep, needs and wishes of various kinds may begin to crop up. And precisely because we are asleep they cannot be satisfied in the ordinary manner of waking life. If we become hungry, we cannot go to the refrigerator and get a snack. If we are thirsty, we can't get a drink of water. Our only recourse, if we are to continue sleeping, is to substitute a memory of a previous satisfaction for the real thing. A nice dream of a juicy hamburger, french fries and a beer might do the trick in this case. Of course, this is only a temporary substitute. Ultimately, we're going to have to satisfy our needs in a more meaningful way.

In this example, the infantile characteristics of the dream are quite straightforward. We have tried to obtain satisfaction for a need by an hallucination, that is to say the dream proper. And we have reverted back to memories of previous moments of gratification of the same need to supply us with the materials for satisfaction.

There is one other item to mention at this point, and that is the reason dreams are primarily visual in nature. Freud conceived of the flow of energy in the brain as moving in one direction during the waking state and in another while we sleep. As we've seen, in the waking state after we receive stimulation of one sort or another, we discharge the energy created through motor activity. If, for example, we were sunbathing on a beach, and felt uncomfortable because of the heat, we would get rid of the discomfort by moving into the shade.

During sleep, the luxury of such movement is not available to us. As a result, energy flows away from motor activity and toward the perceptual end of things.* Returning to our example of the beach, let's suppose we fall asleep in the hot sun. Again we experience the discomfort of the sun beating down on us, but now the energy caused by the discomfort results in information being transmitted toward our perceptual apparatus. This in turn results in a visual experience or a dream—perhaps a dream that we are trying to escape from the fires of hell.

The Stuff of Dreams

By now we have at least an inkling of what Freud considered to be the sources of our dreams, "namely the current wishful impulses that arise during the night."[11] Let's examine how they operate.

Internal, Physical Needs: According to Freud some of these wishes may result in what he called dreams of "convenience." For example, Freud noted that if he ate any highly salted food in the evening, he would develop a thirst during the night which would awaken him.

---

*Freud places some importance on the fact that during sleep the door is shut on the "power of movement"[1] (p. 607). It is interesting to note that there is in reality a loss of muscle tone during REM-sleep dreaming (see chapter 3).

However, his awakening was always preceded by the same dream. He dreamed he was drinking:

> "I dream I am swallowing down water in great gulps, and it has a delicious taste that nothing can equal but a cool drink when one is parched with thirst. Then I wake up and have to have a real drink. This simple dream is occasioned by the thirst which I become aware of when I wake. The thirst gives rise to a wish to drink, and the dream shows me that wish fulfilled. In doing so it is performing a function. . . . I am a good sleeper and not accustomed to be woken by any physical need. If I can succeed in appeasing my thirst by *dreaming* that I am drinking, then I need not wake up in order to quench it. This, then, is a dream of convenience."[12]

Here again, we have an instance of the dream searching out memories of past satisfaction. But because the internal need persists, the dream ultimately can't satisfy the actual need to drink. As a result it is unable to protect sleep.

External Events: In the case of external stimuli, however, which according to Freud are another, though less important, source of dreams, the dream may be more successful in its role as the guardian of sleep. For example, I happen to live in a rather old house. The floors creak as the house shifts or people move about. On the occasion when one of my sons returns home late at night and makes his way past my bedroom door, I might very well dream of being on a boat. Presumably, the stimulus of the creaking floor boards connects with old, fond memories of going to sleep aboard a boat where creaking noises are associated with a gentle, pleasant rocking sensation. In this instance, rather than waking me from sleep, the benign noise of my son walking about the house is presented to me in a fashion totally compatible with continuing to sleep. Of course, if the noise persisted, or if the son in question happened to drop the plate of food he was taking up to his room, I would no doubt be awakened with a start. After all, the dream's ability to preserve sleep against all external intrusions is not limitless, as amply illustrated by a dream Maury[13] reported in 1861.

The setting of Maury's dream was Paris, during the Reign of Terror around 1793. In the dream, he witnessed a number of murders and was himself brought to trial and condemned to be guillotined for his crimes. He was driven in a cart through the streets of Paris past mobs of jeering people. Arriving at the scaffold he slowly mounted the steps. On reaching the top, his hands were bound behind him and he placed his head upon the block. Suddenly, he felt the blade of the guillotine separate his head from his body.

As you might expect, Maury awoke with a start, in extreme anxiety. He discovered that the top of his bed had fallen and had struck him on the neck in just the place the blade of the guillotine would have struck. We'll have occasion to mention this dream in the next chapter when we discuss the length of time it actually takes to have a dream. But for the moment, suffice it to say that in this instance, the dream was not able to preserve Maury's sleep in the face of this rather dramatic intrusion from the external world.

Internal Psychic Impulses: Now let's turn to what Freud considered the primary source of dreams, unconscious impulses or wishes. It is ultimately in the need to guard against the disturbing aspects of these impulses that dreams and their vaunted sleep-protective qualities come to the fore. Yet paradoxically, it's these very impulses that provide the energy for the creation of dreams.

Up to now, the sources of most of the dreams we have discussed seem more or less transparent. Freud's dream of drinking water resulted from thirst incurred as the result of a salty bedtime snack. My dream of a creaking boat was evoked by my son's footsteps in the night.

Maury's dream was brought about by the top of his bed striking him on the neck. So too, we might think, Freud's dream of Irma was brought about by a disturbing encounter with his friend Otto during the day, while Rosette's dream of a solo flight resulted from her recent separation from her husband. But according to Freud, appearances can literally be deceiving.

Freud certainly felt his dream of drinking resulted from his body's need for water. He would no doubt agree that my dream of a creaking boat was induced by the creaking footsteps of my son. And he was sure that Maury's dream was instigated by the top of his bed falling on his neck. As we've said, he believed that dreams can be induced by the body's needs or external events which have the potential to awaken us. The other two dreams are another story altogether.

Freud wrote, "I think it is highly doubtful whether in the case of an adult a wish that has not been fulfilled during the day would be strong enough to produce a dream. . . . *My supposition is that a conscious wish can only become a dream-instigator if it succeeds in awakening an unconscious wish with the same tenor and in obtaining reinforcement from it.*"[14]

Simply put, what Freud meant is that waking experiences, whether they are conscious unfulfilled wishes or wishes of which we are not actually aware, do not have sufficient energy to *cause* a dream. In order to make an appearance in a dream they need to find energy from another source. That source is unconscious, infantile wishes.

He went on to write, "The position may be explained by an analogy. A daytime thought may very well play the part of *entrepreneur* for a dream; but the *entrepreneur*, who, as people say, has the idea and the initiative to carry it out, can do nothing without capital; he needs a *capitalist* who can afford the outlay, and the capitalist who provides the psychical outlay for the dream is invariably and indisputably, whatever may be the thoughts of the previous day, *a wish from the unconscious.*"[15]

Perhaps the simplest way to understand this process is to compare it to the process involved in the formation of dreams driven by external events or somatic needs. If you recall, in the case of somatic needs, dreams may preserve sleep by presenting us with visions of the needs being satisfied. The potentially disturbing stimuli tap past memories of successful satisfaction of similar needs. The dream is an hallucination of our attainment of that satisfaction. Similarly, potentially disturbing external stimuli may be robbed of their disturbing qualities by being connected with past benign or pleasant memories, like those of my creaking boat.

The case of dreams caused by internal, psychic impulses is only slightly different. Events from the day, or the "day residue" as Freud calls them, may connect up with long hidden memories of unfulfilled, infantile wishes. These wishes have been kept under wraps, generally because they are unacceptable or inappropriate. Once tapped by the day residue, these wishes begin to surge toward the surface of consciousness. Because they are unacceptable their arrival at the level of awareness might cause anxiety and threaten the integrity of sleep. To preserve sleep attempts are made to disguise the content of the unconscious thought, to present the dreamer with a scenario that is acceptable to conscious perusal. Insofar as the dreamwork is successful, the dreamer is able to continue sleeping. But just as with internal somatic stimuli and external events, if the unconscious impulses are not adequately disguised they may result in the dreamer ultimately being awakened. In this case, the threat and ultimate awakening arises not from a bodily need or an intrusive external disturbance but from the unconscious memories themselves.

For example, let's take the case of a boy who wished to marry his mother. When he was young, he felt free to express this wish openly. He soon learned, however, that he wouldn't be able to marry his mother. What is more, he discovered that these desires are in fact unacceptable in our society. Now as a young man, he receives an invitation to a friend's wedding. That night, the knowledge of the impending wedding of his friend forms a connection with the dreamer's past desires to marry his mother. Within the Freudian model, awareness of this unconscious wish might well awaken the dreamer. As a consequence, the dreamwork springs into action to present the wish in a disguised fashion, perhaps as an hallucination of the dreamer's own wedding. Here comes the wedding party. There is the dreamer. There is his bride-to-be. There is the dreamer's father. And of course there is his mother. All part of the bridal party in their appropriate roles. All perfectly acceptable.

Within Freud's framework then, the function of dreams as a protection from internal psychic impulses is clear enough. But we might well ask why these psychic impulses try to force themselves into consciousness in the first place. Once repressed, placed under wraps as it were, how can they get out? And if they do try to push their way into consciousness, why is their activity limited to the time when we are asleep?

Freud's answers to these questions are quite straightforward. These psychic impulses are unfulfilled wishes. As such they are constantly seeking fulfillment. They are constantly trying to obtain gratification. They are constantly trying to gain a place in our awareness. Because they are unacceptable wishes we just as constantly have to guard against their appearance or at least their obvious appearance, in our conscious experience.

According to Freud, these wishes attempt to make inroads into our waking lives. He wrote:

The frequent occurrence of conscious daytime phantasies brings these structures to our knowledge; but just as there are phantasies of this kind which are conscious, so, too, there are unconscious ones in great numbers, which have to remain unconscious on account of their content and of their origin from repressed material. Closer investigation of the characteristics of these daytime phantasies shows us how right it is that these formations should bear the same name as we give to the products of our thought during the night—the name, that is, of "dreams." They share a large number of their properties with night-dreams. . . .

Like dreams, they are wish-fulfillments; like dreams, they are based to a great extent on impressions of infantile experiences; like dreams they benefit by a certain degree of relaxation of censorship.[16]*

This relaxation of censorship is central to the answer to our third question. In Freud's view, it is during sleep that censorship is most lax. It is during sleep unconscious psychic impulses are most likely to make headway in their relentless push toward consciousness. It is during sleep our critical facilities, our "watchman," goes to rest permitting our unconscious wishes to "prance upon the stage."[17]

Having said all this, we are obviously hardly closer to discovering the *real* source of either Rosette's dream or Freud's Irma dream.** Oddly enough, we probably can more reasonably guess the source of Rosette's dream

---

*For a detailed exposition of Freud's view of the relationship of waking phantasy to infantile experience see Freud, S. (1947) *Leonardo Da Vinci: A study in Psychosexuality,* New York: Modern Library.

**For an interesting reinterpretation of Freud's Irma dream see Greenberg, R. and Pearlman, C. (1978) If Freud only knew: A reconsideration of psychoanalytic dream theory. *The International Review of Psychoanalysis,* 5, 71–75.

Freud and Dreaming 29

within a Freudian framework than we can the source of-
Freud's dream of Irma. This is because Rosette has provided us with some particularly relevant information,
something Freud either could not or would not do.

Knowing what we do about Rosette's history, we can
speculate that at some time when she was young she may
have heard her mother mention her dead sister. Or else, as
she later told me, in some way Rosette had an awareness
of her sibling because she was treated as a "second child,"
living in the shadow of the memories of her sister. Perhaps
recognizing or feeling a pervasive sadness in her mother,
she wished her sister had never been born. Perhaps she
resented her sister for having a special place in her
mother's memories. And so forth. In short, we can
reasonably hypothesize that Rosette has repressed some
unacceptable thoughts about her dead sister.

Rosette has told us nothing about her daytime experiences prior to having her dream. But within the Freudian context we might speculate that a waking event, the
"entrepreneur," had somehow connected with the past
hidden memories surrounding her sister's death. These
day residues in turn made use of the energy, the
"capital," from the hidden wishes to develop her dream.

Of course, it's impossible to know if our speculations
are correct. Later on we'll have occasion to explore some
dreams obtained in our laboratory that are more clearly
linked to early childhood experiences by the dreamers
themselves. But for the moment, the correctness of our interpretations is less important than understanding the
process of dream formation Freud suggested takes place.
It is, after all, within the framework of Freud's conceptualization of dream formation that we are best able to
understand his view of the function of dreams.

Freud unequivocally stated the primary function of
dreams is to protect the sanctity of sleep. As we have seen,
Freud suggested dreams perform this function in two different yet similar ways. First, they connect potentially
disturbing external and somatic events with past
memories designed to rob those events of their sleep

disturbing qualities. Second, they alter the form of unacceptable memories so they are presented in a relatively benign fashion to the dreamer, once again robbing a stimulus (this time an internal psychic one) of its potential to disturb sleep.

Understanding the processes of dream formation and function as Freud has elucidated them is important for a couple of reasons. First, as we've already mentioned, many aspects of his notions can be seen in a number of subsequent theories concerning the function of dreams. In particular Freud's idea that during dreaming current experiences in some way connect up with past memories is a theme that we will find prevalent in the so called "mastery"[18] notions of dreaming.

These notions suggest that dreams aid us in dealing with contemporary stress. There are a number of variations on the mastery theme which we'll get to later on. However, a common premise running through the various mastery hypotheses is that dreams aid in the solution of present day problems by enabling the dreamer to form connections between current disturbing events and past successful solutions to similar problems.

Second, Freud's ideas about the function of dreams have provided impetus for many of the more recent investigations of dreaming as well as having had profound implications for the direction of research in the area. Since the publication of *The Interpretation of Dreams*, there have been a large number of studies that have tried to test the veracity of Freud's propositions about the *function* of dreams. These studies have used Freud's notions as a starting point for explorations of dreams and dreaming.

As we'll see in the next chapter, with the discovery of REM sleep in 1953 it became possible to explore dreams in a more systematic and controlled fashion than ever before. As a result, the efforts to unlock the secrets of dreams and dream function were redoubled. Admittedly most of these more recent studies were not designed specifically to test Freud's notions. Nonetheless, some of the findings from these studies have had accidental or serendipitous implications for Freud's ideas about the function of dreams.

In the chapters that follow we'll get a chance to explore these different types of studies. Wherever possible we'll try to use Freud's theory as a point of comparison. Ultimately we'll try to reach our own conclusions as to what the function of dreams may be.

3

Sleep and Dream Research

At about 1:30 in the morning, the fairly regular pattern traced by the battery of pens onto the moving belt of graphlike paper was abruptly broken. The pens began to swing wildly and erratically across the paper, spattering ink on the edges of the electroencephalograph and onto the floor.

The turbulent movement of the pens indicated to me that the subject in the next room was moving about in his sleep. It was less than two hours since I had said goodnight to him over the intercom. It was a little more than ninety minutes since the appearance of sleep spindles on the electroencephalograph had indicated that the subject was asleep.

I hoped that the body movement might herald the beginning of a REM (rapid eye movement) period. I could feel the familiar surge of anticipation. I leaned forward to watch the record more carefully. The pens settled into a pattern similar to, yet slightly different from, the earlier graphic representations of sleep.

The relatively thick line of ink recording muscle activity from the chin of the subject had become somewhat narrower. It signified to me that there was a loss of muscle tone. The tracing of the respiration was marked by irregular peaks and valleys, indicating to me that the regular breathing pattern had given way to one of greater variability. The line of ink recording changes in the penis gauge had begun a slow ascent across the moving paper denoting the beginning of an erection. The recordings from the occipital and frontal lobes of the brain were lower in amplitude than they had been before. I was sure all of these changes marked the onset of a REM period.

Within a couple of minutes, the two pens recording eye activity moved in quick, jagged bursts. They reflected the movement of the subject's eyes, under his closed eyelids.

I waited for about seven minutes. Then I turned on a tape recorder and awakened the subject by sounding a loud buzzer placed next to his pillow in the bedroom. He picked up a bedside telephone connected to an intercom and began to report the following dream:

> . . . Well I was sleeping. Here. And I was dreaming that you were going to . . . when you rang the buzzer . . . you were gonna ask me about King. . . . Well I was wondering why you were gonna ask me. I figured you had somebody else in the room, and you were talking about it. You were seated at the console and the other person was seated at that table. . . . Don't ask me why . . . how you got to the subject of Sgt. Preston. And you wanted to know who his lead dog was. So you both thought it was a wonderful idea if you woke me and asked me . . .[1]

When the dreamer completed his narrative, I began to ask him a series of standardized questions. The questions were designed to encourage him to recall further details of this dream without influencing his report. Or to put it another way, they were intended to get him to say more about his dream without putting words into his mouth. For example, I asked questions like: "Can you describe the dream in any more detail?" or "Was there any color in the dream?" When the dream report was finished, the subject answered a number of standard questions about his feelings during the dream, hung up the phone and returned to sleep.

Scenes such as the one I've just described are not exactly commonplace, but they occur with a surprising degree of frequency nowadays, in hundreds of sleep laboratories throughout the world. In these settings, scientists are trying to understand the process and function of sleeping and dreaming.

When I'm running an experiment, I like to arrive at the laboratory about an hour before the subject. This gives me ample time to warm up the electroencephalograph, check out various pieces of equipment and make the subject's bed. The electroencephalograph, by the way, is the sleep researcher's mainstay. Although imposing in both name and appearance, it is essentially no more than a series of amplifiers which can be used to magnify minute electrical activity that is generated by the brain, the muscles, the eyes and so forth. These amplified impulses are in turn registered by a bank of pens on a constantly moving belt of paper. A single night's recording might cover a thousand feet of paper!

In any case, at an appointed time, usually about an hour before his or her normal bedtime, I go to the front door of the building to meet the subject, who is generally a paid volunteer. My laboratory is on the fifth floor of the psychology department. The two of us wend our way through the darkened, sometimes eerily quiet corridors to the well-lit sleep laboratory. The subject goes into the bedroom and gets into night clothes.

When the subject is ready for bed, I attach a predetermined set of electrodes and gauges to various parts of the head and body. For example, I usually attach tiny electrodes to the head and scalp to record brain activity. I also attach electrodes to the chin to register muscle activity and electrodes on the sides of the eyes to record eye movements. Depending on the nature of the study, I might also attach a thin, mercury-filled strain gauge around the chest and abdomen of the subject to record respiration. A similar gauge might be placed on the penis to record erections and other instruments may be used to record heart rate or changes in body temperature.

Surprisingly, in spite of this array of recording devices attached to their bodies, subjects seldom experience any difficulty in falling asleep. Generally, within fifteen minutes or so of turning off the lights in the bedroom, we are able to begin to map the course of a night's sleep.

THE DISCOVERY OF REM SLEEP

In the early 1950s, Eugene Aserinsky, who was then a graduate student at the University of Chicago, made a remarkable serendipitous discovery. Initially, Aserinsky was intent on studying slow, rolling eye movents in infants while they slept in the hope he could uncover a relationship between eye activity and sleep depth. During the long arduous hours of observing the sleeping infants, Aserinsky noted that there were periods when the eyes were quiescent and other times when they exhibited bursts of movement. What is more, the eye movement bursts seemed to be associated with a *lack* of body movement.

Aserinsky along with Nathaniel Kleitman decided to explore this phenomenon more systematically, this time using adults as subjects instead of infants. However, unlike infants, adults would obviously have trouble falling asleep in a lighted room. In order to get around this difficulty, Aserinsky and Kleitman[2] decided to attach electrodes to their subjects and record their eye movements with an electroencephalograph. They also recorded their subjects' brain waves, pulse and respiration.

What they found was that the rapid eye movements, which I just described, occurred periodically and in conjunction with a number of physiological changes. For example the brain waves exhibited low voltage and fast activity, and heart and pulse rates seemed to speed up. As Kleitman later described it, "These changes suggested some sort of emotional disturbance, such as might be caused by dreaming."[3] It's interesting to note that George Ladd,[4] a philosopher at Yale University, had some seven decades earlier suggested that dreams might be associated with movement of the eyes! On the basis of introspection, he postulated that when we dream our eyes move much as they do during the waking state, while when we are not dreaming, our eyes remain quiescent.

REM SLEEP AND DREAMING

In order to investigate the possibility that these periods of rapid eye movement sleep were in fact related to dreaming, Aserinsky and Kleitman, and later Bill Dement[5] awakened subjects in the midst of their REM periods. They were able to elicit dream recall from approximately seventy percent of those awakenings. Since then numerous investigators have succeeded in replicating these findings in many laboratories throughout the world. Although the amount of dream recall obtained has varied (from about sixty to ninety percent) the basic finding that recall of dreams is regularly obtainable from REM sleep is now a well-substantiated phenomenon.

In fact, I was surprised to discover that the term REM has even found its way into the dictionary: "REM, n; pl. REMs [rapid eye movement] in psychology, the periodic, rapid, jerky movement of the eyeballs under closed lids during stages of sleep associated with dreaming."[6]

With such an apparently fine index of dreaming, the next questions to be answered were when and how often do we dream during the night?

THE SLEEP CYCLE

Dement and Kleitman were the first to tackle the daunting task of mapping an entire night's sleep. While earlier work had relied on the use of samples of electroen-

cephalograph recordings taken at various times during
the night, Dement and Kleitman recorded 126 complete
nights of sleep from thirty-three adult subjects. Using a
new categorization procedure, they were able to identify a
sequence of patterns of electrical activity which occurred
over and over again throughout the night. Since then,
large numbers of subjects have spent thousands of nights
in sleep laboratories around the world. Despite this
geographic dispersion and the variable settings in which
recordings were made, sleep patterns have proven to be
remarkably consistent.*

Before getting around to describing what these patterns are like, let me give you a quick course on how we
classify different stages of sleep. It's really not a very complicated procedure. In fact, we often show our subjects
their sleep records when they are finished participating in
a study. We've found that after a brief explanation and a
little bit of practice they become quite proficient at identi-
fying the various stages of sleep. However, to the
uninitiate viewing a sleep record for the first time, it would
probably seem impossible to make any sense out of the
morass of squiggles the pens have spewed out on the electroencephalograph or EEG paper.

To identify brain waves, basically all we do is count.
We count the number of cycles per second occurring at a
given time. That is we count the number of marks made
by a particular pen between lines printed on the EEG
paper. Since the EEG paper is moving at a fixed rate of
speed it is a simple matter to calculate the "speed" (or
cycles per second) of a particular wave. So a fast wave,
such as a *beta* wave which occurs at more than 15 cycles
per second will be represented by a lot of little marks in a
short space on the EEG paper. On the other hand, a slow

---

*The consistent pattern I'm about to describe is characteristic
of adults between approximately twenty and fifty years of age.
The amount of time spent sleeping as well as the composition
of sleep is different, for example, in the very young and the
very old.

wave such as a *delta* wave which has a frequency of under 3.5 cycles per second, will correspondingly be represented by only a couple of marks in the same space of the paper.

As a person sleeps the constellation of brain waves is altered in a characteristic manner. These changes are often accompanied by other events which are also reflected on the electroencephalogram. For example, movement of the entire body may herald a change in the stage of sleep. There are also the more dramatic events associated with REM sleep such as variability in respiration and heart rate, loss of muscle tone, the occurrence of erections and of course the movements of the eyes themselves. As a person begins to fall asleep respiration and heart rates start to slow and the eyes begin to roll in a languorous fashion under closed lids. There is a fairly rapid and smooth descent down through sleep stages 1 and 2 into stages 3 and 4. These latter stages and particularly stage 4 are generally considered to be the deepest stages of sleep. Stage 4 is characterized by a predominance of the delta waves which I described before. It is especially difficult to arouse the sleeping person from this stage of sleep.

After about thirty of forty minutes in stage 4, there is often a body movement as the person turns over or shifts about in bed. The movement generally indicates the beginning of an ascent back through stages 3 and 2. Finally, perhaps heralded by another body movement, the regular respiration and heart rate gives way to more irregular activity. The larger muscles of the body are unable to move although twitches may be apparent in the extremities such as the fingertips. In males, erections begin to occur. The brain waves are much faster than those observed in the deeper stages of sleep. And finally, there are periodic bursts of eye movements. The sleeper is in the midst of a REM period.*

---

*The paradox of great activation of the autonomic nervous system accompanied by the "paralysis" of the larger muscles has occasioned some researchers to call REM sleep "paradoxical sleep."

And by the way, eye movements are readily observable without any fancy equipment. For example, you can see the slow, rolling movements of the eyes under closed lids as a person begins to fall asleep. Similarly, it's possible to observe their fast, conjugate eye movements as they enter a REM period. In fact, anyone who has a cat or dog probably has observed both slow wave sleep and REM periods at one time or another. During slow wave sleep, the animal breathes regularly and is relatively inert. At the onset of a REM, its breathing becomes irregular, its paws, tail and whiskers might twitch, and of course there are bursts of rapid eye movements.

Now returning to our laboratory sleeper, we find that after five or ten minutes in REM a descent toward stage 4 begins. The cycle which has taken about ninety minutes to complete has started again. And indeed, these ninety minute cycles will recur throughout the night, but their composition will be altered. As the night progresses, less and less time is spent in stages 3 and 4 sleep and more and more time is spent in REM sleep. In fact, the last REM period of the night can be more than an hour in length! What this means is that most of our deep sleep, or slow wave sleep, takes place in the first third of the night, while most of our REM sleep takes place in the last third of the night.

As we'll see later on, this remarkably consistent sleep pattern may hold some clues as to the importance of slow wave sleep. It also may play some role in determining which dreams we are likely to recall. But there are other questions we have to deal with first. Remember we said earlier that dreams are readily obtainable when we awaken subjects from REM sleep and that consequently it appears to be an ideal indicant of dreaming. And now we know that REM periods occur regularly throughout the night. In fact, if we sleep between six and nine hours a night, we can expect to have anywhere from four to six REM periods, occupying anywhere from twenty to twenty-five percent of our total sleep time!

To put it another way, dreams seem to be an inevitable and inexorable part of the sleep cycle. It appears as if we dream from four to six times a night and we may spend anywhere from an hour and a half to over two hours dreaming during the night. Or do we?

DREAM TIME AND REAL TIME

The question of how long dreams are, that is how long they are in real time, is not a simple one to answer. Don't forget Maury's dream which I described earlier (chapter 2). Maury speculated his dream must have been caused by the top of his bed hitting his neck. Despite its lengthy content, he inferred it must have occurred in the interval between the blow and his awakening. On the basis of this experience, Maury came to the conclusion that the length of dreams in actual time is extremely short, with many events often being telescoped into a relatively brief interval.

For the dream researcher, Maury's account is interesting but not convincing. Clearly, the report of one event, which could have been embellished in the twenty years intervening between its occurrence and the time the book was written, is tenuous at best.

Most of us have experienced moments when we felt as if we had dreamed for a long period of time before awakening. We also probably have experienced instances where we felt as if our dreams had been extremely short in length. Do our short dreams then come from short REM periods? Do our long ones occur during long REM periods? Or as Maury might have suggested, can lengthy dreams be developed in only a fragment of a REM period? In order to investigate these questions, Dement and Kleitman[7] hit upon the idea of awakening subjects either five or fifteen minutes after the beginning of a REM period, obtaining a dream report, and then asking the subjects to decide if they had been dreaming for either five or fifteen minutes. As it turned out, most of the subjects' judgments as to how long they had been dreaming corresponded to the length of time they had been in REM sleep. In addition, there was a correspondence between the length of the dream narratives and the length of the REM periods from which they were obtained.

But were these results conclusive? Did they really show that we dream *all* the time we have REM periods? The philosopher Norman Malcolm[8] certainly didn't think so. He argued that since the dreamer and the experimenter have only the dreamer's account of the experience in common, there is no basis for making a judgment about the actual length of a dream or even when it took place. Malcolm's argument emphasized one of the difficulties intrinsic to dream research which I alluded to in the first chapter. The dream is unlike events that take place when we are awake. When we are awake, both you and I can observe the same event. We can measure its duration by referring to a clock. In sleep, only the dreamer has access to the events of the dream, and he or she certainly has no clock with which to measure the passage of time.

So, according to Malcolm, it is quite possible both long and short dreams have actually taken place during equally short segments of REM periods. The dreamer might in reality be making his or her judgments of time on the basis of the length of the dream narrative or some other criterion rather than on the basis of the actual length of time spent dreaming. In order to meet the thrust of Malcolm's argument, both the dreamer and the observer have to somehow be supplied with a common reference point in real time. Two studies I know of have met this requirement.

In one the experimenters were interested in exploring the effects of different external stimuli on dreams. They used a water spray, a light and a tone as the stimuli. If the subjects happened to report a dream that exhibited incorporation of one of the stimuli, the experimenters measured the interval between the stimulation and the awakening and tried to calculate the time needed for the events to actually take place. They found that, "In each of the 10 instances, where the stimulus was incorporated and the subsequent interval was precisely timed, the amount of dream action in the interval between the modifying stimulus and the awakening did not vary from the amount of action that would have been expected to take place during an identical time in reality."[9]

In another study,[10] I tried to deal with this question in a similar but more systematic fashion. I used a series of painless shocks to the wrist as a stimulus to provide the dreamer and me with a common reference point in time. I gave the stimulation during REM periods and awakened the dreamer either thirty seconds or three minutes after the stimulation ended. The subjects were instructed to report immediately on what had been going through their minds just before they were awakened.

In those instances when I could identify the presence of the stimulus in the dream report, I asked the subjects to estimate if those events had occurred "more nearly thirty seconds before the awakening buzzer or more nearly three minutes before the awakening buzzer." Let me give you a couple of examples, taken from different subjects, of dreams where incorporation clearly occurred:

> . . . I started walking back here to tell you about it. I metcha in the hall and I told you, Hey, Dave, this thing is. . . . I'm feeling the electrical impulses without the electricity going through. I felt it three or four times. On my left hand . . . then I realized I was in my underwear all along. . . .[11]

> . . . About this place here. That I was in this place and after I came from the rest room I told you that my left hand was very active. And I quoted to you saying that it's active without the whadyacall, without electricity. . . .[12]

So, in the first instance, for example, I asked the question, "Did you feel the electrical impulse more nearly thirty seconds before the buzzer sounded or more nearly three minutes before the buzzer sounded?" In eleven of the twelve instances where the stimulus was incorporated into the dream, subjects judged it as having occurred at a time corresponding to the actual time of the stimulation.

These results, taken together with the others I've described, seem to indicate that not only do we dream when we are in REM sleep, but that we dream *all* during REM sleep. What this means is that rather than dreams being random, fleeting events, they are sometimes lengthy episodes which occur regularly during the night.

What is more, people do report some sort of mental activity after being awakened from non-REM* sleep as well as when they are awakened from REM sleep. As we'll see in the next chapter, the content of non-REM reports is often identified as being more thoughtlike rather than "dreamy." Nonetheless, at least after some non-REM awakenings people do report that they had been dreaming.

When you think of it, it's rather startling to realize we dream *at least* four or five times every night, often more. This information raises a number of interesting questions. The first set of questions has to do with dream formation itself. Is Freud's notion that most dreams are the products of a fortuitous melding of day residues and infantile wishes really tenable? Can these regularly occurring dreams really be *caused* by chance bodily disturbances or external events happening during sleep?

A second set of questions has to do with our apparent lack of ability to remember our dreams. Under normal circumstances, that is when we are sleeping at home, we are only able to remember on average one dream every two

---

*Non-REM is the term used to describe all the stages of sleep that are not REM sleep, that is, stages 1, 2, 3 and 4.

nights.[13] That means we generally forget about eight or nine dreams every two nights! Why is our memory for dreams so fragile? Are some dreams more likely to be remembered than others? If so, why?

Before considering these questions, however, there are a number of other problems worthy of our attention. For example, what exactly are the differences between material obtained from REM and non-REM sleep? And what of the peculiar constellation of events surrounding REM sleep? Does it bear any relationship to our dreams? Do the movements of our eyes indicate we are following the images of our dreams? Does the respiratory irregularity reflect physical exertion or anxiety in our dreams? Does the occurrence of erections indicate men are having erotic dreams? And so forth. We'll consider these questions in the next chapter.

4

Explorations of Dreaming

As we saw in the last chapter, early studies of dreaming indicated that most if not all dreaming takes place during REM sleep. Although some dreams were obtained from non-REM sleep, Dement and Kleitman[1] felt they were merely memories from previous REM periods. This notion was bolstered by the fact that most of the dreams obtained from non-REM sleep were recalled if the awakening had taken place in close proximity to a REM period.

However, subsequent studies of non-REM recall[2] yielded a much higher percentage of dream reports than had previously been obtained—although the amount of recall of dreams from non-REM sleep was still clearly less than that obtained from REM sleep.

The apparent discrepancies between the results of these studies can readily be explained by the different criteria used to define dreams. The earlier investigations required that content be coherent and detailed in order for it to be designated as a dream. The later studies used a much less stringent definition of dreaming and designated the recall of any specific content as a dream.

In any case, the possibility that non-REM dreams are merely memories of REM-period dreams was ultimately laid to rest. It was found that dreams could be obtained even from those non-REM periods that precede the first REM period of the night.[3]

So this new information indicated that dreams are not confined to REM periods. They may occur all throughout the night! It was hard to know what to make of this, especially since, as we noted earlier, REM sleep is such a hotbed of physiological activity. Consequently, the next step was to explore the possibility that REM-sleep dreams differ in some way from those of non-REM sleep.

REM AND NON-REM DREAMING

To explore possible qualitative differences between REM and non-REM dreams, Rechtschaffen and his colleagues simply asked their subjects questions about the reports obtained from REM and non-REM awakenings. As was the case in the other studies, their subjects had more difficulty in recalling dreams from non-REM sleep than from REM sleep. But in addition, Rechtschaffen and his colleagues found subjects tended to characterize their dreams from these different states of sleep differently: "In summary, as compared with REM mentation, subjects report NREM [non-REM] mentation as more poorly recalled, more like thinking and less like dreaming, less vivid, less visual, more conceptual, under greater volitional control, more plausible, more concerned with contemporary lives, occurring in lighter sleep, less emotional and more pleasant."[4]

Attacking this problem from another direction, Monroe[5] and his colleagues found some additional evidence that REM and non-REM dream content are different from each other. They asked judges to categorize dreams obtained from various stages of sleep as having come from REM or non-REM sleep. They found that judges could make the discrimination between the two types of dream content with a high degree of accuracy.

But perhaps the most exciting and innovative research in this area involves attempts to have the dreamers themselves inform you that they are dreaming *while* they are dreaming. I know of a few studies that have tried this type of communication and they're certainly worth noting.*

In one study,[6] the researchers asked people to signal whether they were dreaming or not by pressing a microswitch attached to their index fingers. In the other study,[7] people who identified themselves as being adept at recognizing they are dreaming *while* they are in the midst of a dream** were chosen to be subjects. They were asked to signal the beginning and end of their dreams by specific movements of their eyes. The results of the first study were equivocal at best, but in the second study, subjects signaled the beginning and end of their dreams at times corresponding to the beginning and end of REM periods.

Finally, there is one other study I should mention in this context. In that study,[8] monkeys were placed in a modified telephone booth. They were trained to press a bar more than 3000 times an hour while awake every time images were flashed on a screen in front of them. After falling asleep, the monkeys would periodically engage in furious bar pressing activity while exhibiting the typical REM-period behavior I described in the last chapter. Evidently, they were experiencing visual images during their REM sleep.

In sum then, it appears that dreams as we might typically define them—relatively vivid, hallucinatory, visual experiences, often charged with emotion—are in fact *usually* associated with REM sleep. On the other hand, mental activity during non-REM sleep generally seems to be more like waking thought—more conceptual

---

*There is one other study of a slightly different genre that I'll describe later when we discuss commerce with the environment during sleep. In that study, the experimenter tried to train his subjects to actually report dreams when they were presented with a particular external stimulus during the course of their REM periods.

**These people are often referred to as "lucid" dreamers.

and less emotional in nature. In addition, the products of REM sleep are more likely to be identified as dreams by the dreamers themselves than are the products of non-REM sleep. These findings in turn raised some intriguing questions, which I alluded to in the last chapter.

As I mentioned earlier, when REM sleep was discovered, researchers were struck by the accompanying constellation of physiological activity. Indeed it was this very activity that added fuel to their speculations that REM sleep was associated with dreaming. Once it was established that we do indeed dream regularly during REM sleep, questions about those physiological characteristics and their relationship to dreaming came to the fore.

First among these questions, of course, was one having to do with the movements of the eyes themselves. Simply put, did they move as the dreamer attempts to follow the visual imagery in the dream? Then there were questions surrounding the variability in respiration and heart rate that occurs during REM sleep. Was this variability associated with increased emotionality in dreams? And finally there was the question of the erections that almost invariably accompany REM periods in men. Might they be associated with erotic dream content?

Answers to these questions would be of considerable interest for a couple of reasons. For one thing, they would enable us to better understand the relationship between the psychology and physiology of dreaming. But from the dream researcher's standpoint there was a second, and perhaps more compelling, reason for trying to establish that a relationship exists between physiological events that accompany dreams and the dream content itself. If we were able to say with certainty, for example, that every time there is respiratory variability in a dream, the dream is an anxious one, or every time there is an erection, the dream is an erotic one and so forth, then we would be able to map a night's dreaming without ever waking the subject! We would have a somewhat objective measure of dream content. Of course we wouldn't know what the *ex-act* content of the dreams was. But we would know something about the content and the emotion and the visual imagery of the dreams. And we would know these things without having to disturb our subjects.

DREAMING AND REM-SLEEP ACTIVITY

As we've already noted, since dreams are in large part visual experiences, it seemed logical to speculate that the eye movements reflect a scanning* of the imagery occurring during dreams. The periods of ocular quiescence that occur throughout all REM periods were thought to reflect moments when the dreamer was staring at an object or perhaps looking at something far away in the dream. For example, in the waking state, if we watch television or look at an airplane high up in the sky our eyes move very little if at all.

In order to test the scanning hypothesis, Dement and Kleitman recorded both vertical and horizontal eye movements during REM periods. They awakened their subjects and obtained dream recall immediately after a distinctive eye movement pattern had occurred. For example, one dream they obtained involved purely horizontal eye movements. In that dream, the dreamer was observing people hurling tomatoes at one another. In another instance, this time involving purely vertical movements of the eyes, the dreamer reported he had been climbing up ". . . a series of ladders looking up and down as he climbed."[9]

In a subsequent, more sophisticated study, other researchers tried to actually *predict* the nature of the eye movement patterns on the basis of the dream narrative. When the subjects rated their dream recall as being vivid,

---

*For obvious reasons this notion became known as the "scanning hypothesis."

the experimenters were able to predict the direction of the eye movements throughout the dream approximately eighty percent of the time. For example, one subject reported:

> Right near the end of the dream I was walking up the back stairs of an old house. I was holding a cat in my arms. . . . I walked up as a dancer would, holding my head high, and I glanced up at every step I took. [There were] five or six [steps]. I reached the head of the stairs and I walked straight over to a group of people about to begin a circle dance. . . . I looked straight ahead at the person across from me. Then I woke up.[10]

In this instance, the experimenter correctly predicted there would be five vertical upward movements as the dreamer walked up the stairs and a few horizontal movements when she reached the top.

These results, as well as those of a more recent study[11] which found that judges could match dream narratives with the general direction of the recorded gaze of the eyes, were intriguing. However, as is often the case in our line of work, there is other evidence that doesn't seem to be consistent with the scanning hypothesis.

For one thing, as we've already noted, while dreams with predominant visual components are recalled most readily from REM sleep, they do occur during non-REM sleep, which is of course devoid of eye movements. Also congenitally blind people, who have no visual imagery in their dreams, nonetheless exhibit eye movements during REM periods.[12] And finally, a study using a recording technique that allowed the experimenters to know not only the direction of the eye movements but also the focus of the gaze when the eyes were not moving, found that eye movements only occasionally matched the imagery of dream narratives.[13]

A study[14] of the relationship of erections to dream content yielded similar, equivocal results. In that study, one experimenter awakened subjects from sleep at different points in the erection cycle. For example, some awakenings occurred after a sharp increase in erections, others after a sharp decrease, still others after relatively short or long periods of full erections and so forth. Then Charles Fisher, having no knowledge of when the awakenings had taken place, tried to predict the state of the erection on the basis of the dream narrative.

Fisher was most successful in making predictions involving sudden, sharp decreases and increases in the erections. Seven dreams associated with sharp detumescence were marked by the presence of anxiety, five of them containing aggression directed toward the dreamer. On the other hand, four of the five dreams associated with sharp increases in tumescence contained overtly erotic episodes. However, Fisher was much less successful at predicting the state of the erection when the awakenings occurred from the less dramatic moments of the cycle, as it were. So in sum, these results suggested that at times there may be some relationship between the nature of the erection and the dream content, but that it is by no means a constant one.

As we might expect, studies of the relationship between respiration and heart rates and dream content yielded results similar to those found in the studies of eye movements and erections. For example, in one study,[15] some evidence of a relationship was found between heart rate variability and emotionality in REM-period dreams.

In another study,[16] this one focusing on respiration and dream content, Hobson and his colleagues obtained dream reports after periods of specific respiratory patterns during both REM and non-REM sleep. The four patterns of respiration they chose were: regular breathing; variable breathing; rapid, shallow breathing; and periods of apnea.*

---

*Apnea describes a breathing pattern in which the sleeping person exhales, and doesn't inhale for a fairly long period of time. Breathing patterns of this type have been implicated in some sleep disorders.

The authors were able to find some instances in which the respiratory pattern corresponded to the dream narrative. Take the following dream reported immediately after a brief episode of apnea:

> . . . I was dreaming . . . uh, that . . . uh . . . well, it was a play . . . and, uh, a person was being choked. That's exactly when you called my name; . . . a person was being choked . . . and I, by the way, was the actress that was being choked. [Here one of the experimenters asked if there were any emotions connected with the event.] Well, I was just being choked. . . . Uh, I guess fear or something like that.[17]

In this instance, the dreamer's experience in the dream of being choked corresponded to her apneic respiration pattern, as did her apparent anxiety. But as the authors were quick to point out, instances of this type of correspondence between dream narratives and respiratory activity were by no means constant.

In short, it seems quite clear that the one-to-one relationship that we hoped to find between the dream narrative and the accompanying physiology just doesn't exist. Nevertheless, additional findings from this last study coupled with results from other studies suggest that the physiology accompanying dreams may very well coincide with some aspects of the dream report. For example, Hobson and his colleagues noted that reports obtained from both REM and non-REM periods accompanied by high respiratory rates or greater respiratory variability were more likely to be called dreams by the subjects than content obtained from these states when there was little respiratory variability or when the rate of respiration was relatively slow.

What is more, respiratory rate seemed to be related to reports of strong emotions of fear and pleasure in the dreams. These findings are very similar to results from a study of our own.[18] In that study, we found higher respiration rates to be related to an increase in hostility, depression and anxiety in dreams. We also found that dreams containing greater amounts of hostility and anxiety were often accompanied by a greater number of eye movements than dreams devoid of these emotions. These results in turn dovetailed nicely with those from other studies. For example, eye movement activity has been shown to be related to such dream attributes as bizarreness, vividness, emotionality, aggression and intensity.[19]

So what does this all mean? I think what it means is that there is some general relationship between dream content and its accompanying physiology. It seems reasonable to assume that when we dream of events that are particularly emotionally charged, those events activate our autonomic nervous systems much as they would during the waking state. For example, if we were anxious while awake, we might very well breathe at a more rapid rate. Similarly, anxiety, or at any rate emotionality, in dreams might also cause us to breathe more rapidly.

The increased number of eye movements that often accompany highly emotional dreams might be best understood by another analogy to events occurring in the waking state. There is evidence, for example, that people look away from threatening aspects of pictures when they are awake.[20] It is not unreasonable to assume a similar process might well take place when the visual imagery of dreams is particularly threatening.

Finally, if we continue with our analogy to the waking state, it is perhaps not altogether surprising that the relationship between physiological events and dream content is not as constant as we had hoped. For one thing, in the waking state we don't respond to all emotional experiences in an identical fashion. There are no doubt instances of emotionality when only some of our autonomic responses are aroused. For another, as we[21] and others[22] have pointed out, different individuals have characteristically different ways of responding to emotional events during the waking state. Consequently, it would be reasonable to expect different types of responses to emotionality in dream content from different individuals.

This brings up some interesting, related questions. First of all, do dreams of the night reflect or respond to events that take place during the day? That is, is there some sort of continuity between our waking and sleeping experiences?* If such a continuity exists, how is it manifested? Do elements from daytime activities find their way directly into dreams? Or do they appear in some disguised fashion? Are emotional or stressful daytime experiences more likely to have an impact on dream formation than neutral or benign ones?

In addition to being interesting and important questions in their own right, these questions also of course have implications for Freudian theory (chapter 2). As you no doubt recall, Freud believed that daytime experiences are a relatively unimportant part of dream formation. According to him, they merely provide the setting for the representation of internal, psychic experiences in dreams. Consequently, he would have expected little difference in the amount of representation in dreams of striking or emotionally laden experiences and benign daytime events.

Within the framework of the notion of continuity between our waking and sleeping lives there are a couple of compelling questions that have to be answered. First, are the emotions of the day reflected in the emotions of our dreams? Simply put, if we go to sleep with upsetting events on our minds, will our dreams reflect this disturbing state of affairs? And second, does the physiology and pattern of sleep itself reflect the emotionality of our wak-

---

*The possibility that there is continuity between our waking experiences and dream content is referred to as the "continuity hypothesis."

ing experiences? That is, do the patterns of sleep remain constant regardless of our daytime experiences or might they be altered in some manner because of them? I'll consider these questions in the next chapter.

5

Daytime Events, Sleep and Dreaming

As we saw in the last chapter, there are some interesting and important questions that have to be answered about the impact waking experience may have on the nature of both our sleep and dreams. These questions not only have some theoretical implications which I've already mentioned, but they have practical implications as well.

If, let us say, we were to find that certain types of waking experiences altered dream content in a negative way or disturbed sleep, we might want to take some steps to reduce this disruption. For example, if we discovered that mulling over stressful events before bedtime interfered with sleep or resulted in anxiety-ridden dreams, we might attempt to counter these effects by engaging in a relaxing activity before going to bed. Or if we discovered that engaging in certain types of presleep activity resulted in distressing dreams or disturbed sleep, we might avoid them.

But how to go about getting answers to these questions? There are a number of possibilities. One possibility would be to find people who are undergoing stressful experiences in their lives, bring them into the laboratory, record their sleep and collect their dreams. The advantage of this approach is that stressful events occurring in the course of one's life are no doubt more meaningful and hence more stressful than anything we could invent in the laboratory. If the sleep of these stressed people turned out to be disturbed and/or their dreams reflected their daytime concerns, we might be able to make some cautious statements about the effects of such stressful events on sleep and dreams.

The disadvantage of this approach is that our statements would necessarily be cautious because we would have no *real* comparison group for our subjects. We could merely say that our subjects' sleep was different, let's say, from that of other people of a similar age group. And we might speculate this was a result of the stress they were undergoing in their waking lives. Similarly, we might speculate that the dream content or a high level of emotionality in the dreams of our subjects resulted from their waking concerns. These are probably reasonable speculations, but they are not as neat and clear-cut as we would like them to be.

Well, of course there are other possibilities. One thing we might try would be to bring people into the laboratory and confront some of them with a stressful experience, while providing other subjects with a similar but benign experience. Again we would record their sleep and collect their dreams. In this case, if the people who had the stressful presleep experience had more disturbed sleep or if their dreams were more emotional than those of people who experienced the benign presleep event, we could make the same speculations as we did before with a little more vigor and confidence. We could say, look, this group of people had a disturbing waking experience. The other group had a similar experience that was not disturbing. The first group had sleep patterns and/or dream content that was different from that of the second. We feel that the different waking experiences were the *causes* of the differences we found in sleep.

Still a third possibility, which is really a variant of the one we just discussed, is to give the *same* people different waking experiences. Just as I described before, we would give our subjects a stressful presleep experience prior to their bedtimes on one night. Before bedtime on another night, we would give the same subjects a benign or neutral presleep experience. In this way, we would be comparing the sleep and dreams of the same people after they had different presleep experiences. Again, if disturbed sleep or emotional dreams appeared after the stressful waking experience and not after the benign one, we would have some confidence in asserting the waking stressful events *caused* the disruption of sleep and the alteration of dream content.

However, as I implied, there are problems associated with inducing stress in the manner I've described. One of the major problems is finding a stimulus that is *truly* stressful for a number of different people. And once having found such a stressful stimulus, there is the problem of finding a matching but benign stimulus to use for a comparison. Nonetheless, as we'll see, dream researchers have more or less been able to surmount these problems.

As you've probably noticed, all of the studies I've just outlined are predicated on people sleeping in the laboratory instead of in their homes. There are some obvious advantages to doing it this way. For one thing we would be able to record any physiological changes accompanying stress. But probably the most important advantage is we would almost certainly be able to capture a number of dreams from each night.*

However, doing dream research in the laboratory is not without its drawbacks. As we noted earlier, the laboratory is a peculiar and generally sterile environment. Subjects are asked to go to sleep with a number of elec-

---

*As I've noted, on average we remember only one dream every two nights at home. Yet, by awakening people during their REM periods in the laboratory, we can obtain four or five dreams on a given night. I'll discuss some of the reasons for this difference in recall later on.

trodes stuck to their bodies. What is more, they are observed while they are asleep and they know they are going to be awakened a number of times during the night. Might this unusual situation not itself have an impact on sleep and dream content?

Interestingly enough, a couple of studies,[1] found the first night in the laboratory often resulted in subjects spending more time awake, having less REM sleep and having more periods of arousal than on subsequent nights. Similarly, other studies,[2] revealed that dreams recovered from subjects during their first night in the laboratory were marked by a relatively large number of representations of the experimental situation. Subsequent examinations,[3] of the so-called "first night effect" demonstrated that by providing a "hotel-like" atmosphere as opposed to a more clinical, sterile environment, the sleep pattern on the first night in the laboratory became similar to that of any other night. However, the dreams of the first night still contained a greater number of representations of the laboratory environment than did dreams of subsequent nights.

This problem could obviously be ameliorated to some extent by allowing our subjects to have a practice night in the laboratory. We could provide them with a night to become accustomed to their surroundings. But the discovery of the first night effect is itself instructive. Right from the start, it suggests that both dreams and sleep are relatively sensitive entities. It suggests they both are responsive to changes in the environment.

Another thing I should mention in this context is even though we can reduce the first night effect by providing a night of adaptation, references to the laboratory often reappear when we begin an experiment and particularly when we introduce a stressful presleep event. This is no doubt because the laboratory as well as the experimenters themselves become associated in the dreamer's mind with the stressful event.

Having said all this, the advantages of bringing subjects into the laboratory and being able to control the nature of their presleep experiences nonetheless seemed to outweigh the disadvantages. However, there have been times when practical considerations such as the enormous cost of doing dream research in the laboratory or the desire to explore the impact of "real life" experiences on dreams have resulted in researchers eschewing the controlled laboratory environment. I think that's a lucky thing. Our understanding of the relationship between dreams and waking experience has no doubt been enhanced by the fortuitous blending of information from both home and laboratory studies. In the sections that follow, I'll try to group together studies of both types when they are designed to explore the effects of similar stimuli on sleep and dream content. My aim is to give you a feel for how each type of research contributed in its own way to a clearer picture of the intimacy of the relationship between our waking and sleeping lives.

STUDIES OF PRESLEEP EXPERIENCES

Stressful Films

As it turned out, films were found to be a rather useful tool with which to explore the effects of presleep experiences on dreams. For one thing, it's fairly easy to find emotionally charged films. It's also a relatively simple task to find matching benign ones. For another, it's possible to catalogue the on-screen images and use them as "tracers," to see if and how they appear in subsequent dreams.

In one study I worked on at Downstate Medical Center in New York City with my colleagues Don Goodenough, Arthur Shapiro, Helen Lewis and Hy Witkin we chose two rather unusual films as our stressful stimuli. One was an anthropological film of a subincision, a rite of passage of the Arunta, a tribe found in Australia. The other was a film of the birth of a baby in which a Malmstrom Vacuum Extractor was used to aid in the delivery. Each of these films ran for about fifteen minutes. I'll describe these films in more detail a little later on.

To match the subincision film, which was silent and in black and white, we found a silent, black and white travelogue depicting some scenes of London, England. Since the birth film was in color, with a sound track, we chose a travelogue of the western part of the United States which was also in color with an accompanying sound track to match it.

The plan of our study was quite straightforward. We decided to use night workers as our subjects, so that we could maintain our normal daytime schedules. We divided the labor among us. I was responsible for putting the electrodes and respiration gauges on the subjects and showing them the movie. I was also responsible for monitoring their physiological responses while they watched the movie and recording their physiology and sleep patterns while they slept during the night.* Finally, I had to decide when during the REM periods the subjects should be awakened in order to obtain a dream report.

Goodenough and Witkin were responsible for collecting the dreams over an intercom and holding a postsleep interview with the subjects after the last awakening of the night. The dream reports and the postsleep interview were all recorded for subsequent analyses. Helen Lewis was in charge of analyzing the dream content. And Arthur Shapiro was in charge of providing the technological wherewithal to analyze the physiological data by computer rather than by hand. Before going further, let me digress for a moment to give you an idea of the importance this technological advance, then in its infancy, had for us.

As I already mentioned, it takes about 1000 feet of EEG paper to record one night of sleep. In a prior,

---

*"Night" here obviously refers to the time the subjects slept, rather than to the actual time of day.

preliminary study, Goodenough and I would go into the hallway of the ninth floor of the hospital building where our laboratory was located. We would lay out a night's recording in the corridor. Then, rulers in hand, on our knees, we would carefully measure, for example, the distance between the peaks of respiration traced on the paper, searching for periods of respiratory irregularity. Not only did we suffer sore knees and tired eyes, but as you can well imagine, we had to suffer the incredulous comments of the many passersby. Looking back at it now, I can see how two grown men crawling around on their hands and knees in the middle of a hospital corridor might have looked a bit peculiar.

Well at long last, with the aid of the computer, this onerous task was eliminated. The physiological records could be recorded on magnetic tape and a job that had formerly taken us hours to complete could be accomplished in minutes.

But let's get back to the study. Our twenty-eight male subjects were recruited by advertisements in the New York City newspapers. They were to be paid for their participation in the study. They were, as I've already said, night workers: post office employees, employees of the New York City transit system, bakers and so forth.

The design of the study called for our subjects to sleep in the laboratory for five nights, one week apart.* The first night was an adaptation night, to allow them to get used to the laboratory setting. On each of the subsequent nights, the subjects saw one of the four films just prior to going to sleep. In order to make sure our stressful

---

*When dreams are collected a number of times during a single night, subjects necessarily undergo some sleep deprivation. Consequently, in order to minimize sleep disturbance in studies such as ours, dream collection nights are typically interspersed with nights of uninterrupted sleep either in the laboratory or at home. In this study, the subjects slept at home between visits to the laboratory.

and neutral films had the desired effects on the emotions of our subjects, we asked them to fill out a questionnaire about their mood both before and after they saw the films.

During the night, the subjects were awakened by a buzzer at every REM period, picked up a phone near their bed and related anything going through their minds just prior to the awakening. Every time there was a dream report the subjects filled out a mood questionnaire to indicate how they felt while they were dreaming. Then they were allowed to go back to sleep. In the morning, they went through an extensive postsleep interview in which they were asked to try to recall all their dreams of the night and to provide us with any associations they might have had to their dreams.

Let me give you examples of some of the dreams we obtained after our stressful films. One of the films, as I've already mentioned, depicted the birth of a baby with the aid of a Malmstrom Vacuum Extractor, an instrument sometimes used instead of forceps. It was a medical training film. In the movie, the subject first saw a description of the vacuum extractor itself along with an explanation of how it worked. Then the scene switched and subject saw a vagina into which was inserted the cup of the vacuum extractor. (The cup was attached to the baby's head which was not yet visible.) Next a hand encased in a rubber glove was seen pulling rhythmically on a wire attached to the cup for some minutes. Then suddenly, in a gush of blood, the baby was born.

After the buzzer rang for the first awakening of one of our subjects, the following interchange* took place between the experimenter (E) and the subject (S):

E: Was anything going through your mind?

---

*In all of the dream transcriptions throughout the book, I've taken the liberty of editing out some of the pauses and repetitions that almost invariably accompany dream reports made following abrupt awakenings in the laboratory.

S: No, I really just, uh, I was dreaming about . . . let me see, a group of college boys walking down the lane, in the lane, in the uh, in the park, singing, and they were outside there in the distance, and there was a group of girls all dressed in white sitting on the park benches, carrying flowers, I think. Um, it was dark and they were covering, uh, they were wearing white gloves . . . they were trying to hide something . . . lots of flowers in the park. Yellow ones I think. Regular flowers.

E: Did you recognize anybody in the dream?

S: No. There's nobody I could recognize.

E: Were you in the dream?

S: No, I wasn't. I couldn't particularly single out anybody I could recognize in the dream. I had to make a special effort to retain the . . . you know, it disappears after a few seconds, if I don't make a constant effort to retain it.

E: Were there any feelings connected with it?

S: No, I guess you might say I was a passive observer of the scene. I had no feelings either way of what was going on. It had been going on maybe a few minutes. I guess then I woke up. At the beginning sometime earlier it had something to do with insects, uh bees. I was catching bees. Somebody was catching bees and letting them go on flowers, you know, pollinating the flowers.

E: Did you say you were catching bees?

S: At first, the beginning there were uh, they were in a laboratory or something being used for experimental purposes. They were being used to pollinate flowers, well that was way back, hard to remember the beginning of the dream. As you go along you get more involved, one thing leads to another. Yes, that's about it, you know. These bees were pollinating these flowers, and they were bright yellow, shining almost in the dark, and these girls didn't want these boys to see them. They didn't want to see them, so they were trying to hide . . . to cover up their elbows and holding their arms so they wouldn't be seen, the gloves wouldn't be seen. The whiteness of the gloves wouldn't be seen in the dark. Way off in the dark you could hear them singing as they were walking along the walks. That's about it.[4]

The theme of birth is nicely represented in this film by images of bees pollinating flowers. The physician's rubber gloves which become strikingly bloodied as the baby emerges, appeared repeatedly in the dream, but were transformed into a less threatening, pristine whiteness. The references to the "laboratory" and "experimental purposes" are examples of the experimental situation itself, charged as it had become by the viewing of the film, also making its way directly into the dream. This was, of course, in spite of our use of an adaptation night to allow our subjects time to acclimatize themselves to the laboratory situation.

Let's take a look at an excerpt from the second dream of the night from the same subject.

E: Okay. Would you tell me anything that was going through your mind?

S: . . . I don't know, at the moment you woke me up I was flying around in the airplane looking out, sort of, like looking out well not through a window, exactly, looking out through like a hole. Well, anyhow, I could see the part of the airplane where the wing is attached, the body of the plane. And just above me and to my left was a hole and through the hole was protruding a coil of wire, and there was a man holding the end of the wire . . . big wire, and he had his finger through the end of it, pulling it, it was attached to . . . the other part of the wire was attached to a door, and when he pulled the wire, the door would go up and down . . . and uh, it was sort of a troop carrier plane, people, parachutists, jumping out of the airplane. . . . Anyway I was explaining it to the other fellow. . . . He was telling me that, uh, about somebody who was making these wires. He went into the business of making these wires. . . . He was telling me about all of his children. . . . I was telling him how many children I had. It seems we had large families, the two of us.[5]

Again we can see an image from the film in the rhythmic pulling of the wire attached to the door of the "troop carrier plane." And the theme of birth was represented here by the discussion of children in the dream.

Let's take a look at one more dream from this study before going on. This dream was collected on the third awakening after the subject had viewed the subincision film. In the film, several episodes of the subincision rite were depicted. During the rite, the undersides of the penises of the young initiates were cut from the tip to the scrotum. The wounds were cauterized over an open fire. Our subject reported that:

One segment of the dream quite ironically dealt with the fact that I walked in with my grandmother into a pet shop and wound up buying a rooster. . . . My grandmother was going to buy the rooster. One of those multicolored things. And of course I was opposed to it on the grounds, only of course that I said, "Well they're very hard to raise, they're dirty," and so forth and so on. She says "Yes" but . . . "look how alert this thing is, they're very smart looking, you know multicolored things." Well we wound up buying it, and uh, plus they bagged it like they would a dead chicken. Uh we finally got this thing in the bag and we waited a few moments and he was out of the bag. He was very ornery. . . . When he was put in a bag he, uh, broke out of the bag and now another party came along and picked him up in the broken bag and all and put him in another bag because, uh, you know, uh, just, uh, in other words, he was just bouncing, trying to get out of this bag.[6]

Well, what to make of this dream? On the surface we could settle for the rooster being a phallic symbol and hence related to the prominent theme of the subincision film, but our subject confirmed the phallic aspect of this dream when he related the following story from his childhood.

When he was a little boy, he in fact used to go shopping for chickens with his grandmother. Describing those times he said:

And she'd go into the chicken coop and pull a chicken out herself and she had to feel it. What she was feeling for I don't know. But she says she could tell whether the chicken's good or not by feeling it. . . . Well it would be Saturday morning and I would go with her. And nobody could get her a chicken. Usually they would have men to pull out the chickens, and the scales would have pieces of string on to tie the wings or legs and weigh the chicken. Well, this didn't happen with my grandmother. She had to go and pull the chicken outa' the coop and feel it, or if in the event he would pull it out, she had to feel it before the man was allowed to weigh it. Of course I don't know what she was feeling for, but if it didn't feel right, back in the cage it went.

When our subject was asked whether he knew at the time what she was feeling for, he replied:

No, she would say in Italian "la ozza," which is the neck or the feedbag in the neck. But she was feeling down somewhere around the stomach, so, uh, she was feeling for something else. Because I don't know whether they feel down [in] that position where the chicken's eggs are, which is right about here. She would tell me it was the chicken's neck. Maybe she was afraid she'd have to go into detail about the boy and girl chicken. I don't know. [Then he laughed.][7]

These dreams are just a sample of the 264 dreams we collected during our study. But they are particularly interesting for a number of reasons. First, they clearly showed that stressful presleep events do find their way into dreams of the night. That is, they demonstrated there is some continuity (chapter 4) between our waking experiences and the content of our dreams. Second, the appearance of the events is not limited to a single dream of a night. Third, the manner in which the presleep event is represented in the dream not only varies from dreamer to dreamer but also may vary from dream to dream, no matter who the dreamer is. And fourth, dreams can, and sometimes do, tap into past childhood memories.

There is one other aspect of our study that's important to mention. Our results indicated there is also some continuity between the nature of the response to the waking experience and the subsequent response during sleep and dreams. For example, while all of our subjects exhibited an increase in dream emotionality after viewing the stressful films, those subjects who reported more anxiety after viewing the stressful films also exhibited more emotionality in their dreams. Similarly, those subjects who exhibited respiratory irregularity while watching the subincision episodes had similar respiratory responses accompanying their dreams on nights following the stressful films. On the other hand, subjects who had no waking respiratory irregularity during the subincision episodes also had none during their dreams.[8]

In sum, our study demonstrated that presleep experiences could alter the content of dreams and their accompanying mood. It also illustrated that the more stressful presleep experiences were more likely to have an impact on both dream content and mood than the neutral presleep events. In addition, it demonstrated that the extent and nature of the responses to these presleep experiences during dreaming are at least in part a function of the particular characteristics of the individual involved. Consequently, those individuals who were most affected by the presleep stimulus had the most emotionally charged dreams. In a like manner, distinctive physiological responses to the stressor in the waking state were mirrored while asleep.

Similar dream content changes were found in other studies. For example, in a different study which also used the subincision film as a presleep stimulus[9] it was found the subjects who were more emotionally aroused when viewing the film were more likely to dream about it than those who were not.

Another study by Roz Cartwright and her colleagues in Chicago provides a rather clear demonstration of how individual differences may ultimately influence the nature of the appearance of presleep events in dreams. In that study,[10] the *same* erotic movie was shown to both homosexual and heterosexual young men. Both of these groups exhibited an increase in incorporation of the laboratory situation into their dreams after viewing the film. However, the heterosexual group had more symbolic and little direct sexual content in their dreams. On the other hand, the dreams of the homosexual group contained a great deal of explicitly sexual material.

In short, this is a lovely illustration of the way in which particular characteristics of specific individuals may mediate the dreamer's response to a particular presleep stimulus. It's quite clear that the meaning of the waking experience to a particular person determines in large part how, or even whether, it will ultimately appear in a dream. This will become even more apparent as we go along. But first, it may be instructive to take a look at the results of a study that attempted to explore the effects of a stressful presleep film on sleep itself.

As I mentioned, our film study did examine some of the physiological changes occurring during sleep. However, as is true with all studies involving dream collection throughout the night, it was not possible to map the pattern of sleep as a whole. This is because the intrusion of the number of awakenings essential for dream collection during a night necessarily alters the normal course of sleep. The only way to examine the effects of presleep events on sleep itself, then, is to present the subjects with charged or neutral experiences before they go to bed and allow them to sleep through the night without any artificial interruption. This is precisely what we did.[11]

On one night, our subjects saw either the subincision film, or its companion film, the London travelogue. On a second night, a week later, they saw whichever film they had not seen the first night. We found that the stress film increased the number of spontaneous awakenings associated with REM sleep as well as increasing the number of REM periods terminated by spontaneous awakenings. We also found an increase in the frequency of eye movements in REM periods following the viewing of the stressful film.

Interestingly enough, as you'll recall (chapter 4), an increase in the number of eye movements is sometimes associated with hostility, anxiety, bizarreness, vividness, aggressiveness, emotionality and intensity of the accompanying dreams. As you can see, all of the effects I've described occurred during REM sleep. Consequently we speculated that the anxiety caused by the subincision film carried over into sleep and dreams and produced a disturbing effect during REM sleep.

Now let's move on to some other types of presleep experiences. Let's see if they too result in alterations of dream content and/or the patterns of sleep.

Stressful Tests

Since many of the people doing research on sleep and dreams work in an academic environment, it was only a matter of time before someone came up with the idea of seeing how tests affect the sleep and dreams of students.

In one of our own studies,[12] we compared the dream content and sleep of two groups of university students. Both groups received tests, which they thought were "intelligence" tests, just prior to bedtime on their third and fourth nights* in the laboratory. The tests in fact were not intelligence tests, but they were constructed of items similar to ones found on typical intelligence and scholastic aptitude tests.** One group received a relatively easy test which they could complete in the allotted time. The second group received a more difficult version of the test which could not be completed in the time they were given. After taking the tests, as you might expect, both groups took longer to fall asleep than they did on the baseline night. On the fourth or dream collection night, subjects who had taken the difficult test exhibited more anxiety and somewhat higher levels of incorporation of the test material than subjects who had taken the easy test.

In a similar study, this one a home dream study,[13] we gave subjects difficult and easy tests and sent them off to their homes with tape recorders. Their job was to awaken themselves one half hour before their normal rising time and record any dreams they were able to recall and assess their mood during the dream. There were a couple of interesting aspects to this study. First of all, in this study we

---

*By now you will have guessed that the first night was an adaptation night to accustom the subjects to the laboratory. The second night was a night of uninterrupted sleep which was used as a comparison night (often called "baseline" night) to see if sleep patterns were altered by the presleep tests.

**It's important to note that in all studies where subjects are in any way misled, there is an extensive debriefing to insure that they understand the purpose of the manipulation and to allay any residual discomfort they may happen to feel.

used essentially the same presleep stimulus as we did in our laboratory study. Yet, the subjects in the home dream study responded differently from those in the laboratory study to our easy test condition.

Our home dream subjects were selected because they were high scorers on a neuroticism scale. People of this nature have been shown to be better at recalling their dreams at home than the general population. As it turned out, these people also responded with greater anxiety to the test situation than the general population would be expected to. As a result, both groups of subjects indicated they were made anxious by the testing procedure. It did not matter whether the test was easy or difficult! Consequently, both groups of subjects exhibited incorporations of the test experience and accompanying anxiety in their dreams.

On the other hand, the laboratory subjects were not selected to be high on neuroticism. As a result, in that study our manipulation worked. That is to say, the subjects who experienced the difficult test felt more anxious after having taken it than the subjects who took the easy test. Consequently, as we have seen, the subjects in the difficult test situation exhibited more anxiety in their dreams than the subjects from the other group. In short, when you compare our home and laboratory studies, you have yet another example of how different people may respond to essentially the same experience in a totally different manner.

The other interesting aspect of our home dream study was that we collected dreams for a somewhat extended period of time. The design of the study called for our subjects to come to the laboratory and receive their instructions and a tape recorder. Then they had a practice (or adaptation) night of dream recording followed by a baseline (or comparison) night of dream recording. Finally, the test was administered and the subjects recorded their dreams for six more consecutive nights. Here are some dream samples from a couple of subjects.

The first dream is taken from a baseline night before the subject received the test. It is a nice example of how the general experimental situation often finds its ways into dreams:

> The dream I had last night was quite like the experiment I'm doing now. . . . I remember sitting in a chair . . . and I know I was supposed to record all the dreams or hallucinations I had . . . but there were two kinds of dreams or hallucinations, they were in color or black and white. The ones I was to record were in color. . . . I do remember these. . . . So I recorded less hallucinations or dreams than actually happened. . . . And I wasn't supposed to sleep and then to wake up and do it in the morning like I do now . . . I just sit in a chair and after some time . . . I would record what happened to me . . . or at least what I dreamed happened to me . . . I do remember recording one dream or whatever I had . . . `in the experiment during my dream and that was I was at a big party. . . . There was a large backyard, a large house, and a pool. . . . It was sort of like the kind of parties that you see in the movies. . . . Everyone's just standing around drinking cocktails . . . getting very drunk and I think I'm just watching this from above. I'm not really part of this. I'm just watching everyone have a good time . . . I'm not in the house. I'm just more or less up in the sky looking down at the pool, looking at everyone and all I can hear is a faint mumbling. I can't really tell what's going on.*

The next dream, from a different subject, occurred three nights after he received the stressful test:

---

*Dream reports that are not referenced in this book have been culled from narratives that have never been published before.

I dreamt that I was in a classroom . . . I was writing a test and somehow I didn't know the test. I just sat there . . . I couldn't think of anything in the test. It was like a totally different test. It's like I'd never seen the material in my life. People were looking at me and the teacher was wondering what I was doing. Basically this was the dream.

And here's a dream from the same subject five nights after he took the stressful test:

It was a short dream again. I couldn't think of anything. I was in . . . I had written an exam . . . I guess for one of my subjects . . . in uh I think it was university. . . . And it was like I studied the day before and I wrote the test. I mean I took the test and any question was just like foreign to me. Everything was totally blank. And the thing about it is that . . . the dream was uh . . . I knew about it. It's like I kept saying to myself, "Oh, it's all right, I'm going to wake up anyway. It's only a dream." I kept on saying, "It's only a dream," which is really weird for me. I was the one taking part in it.

So here again we have examples of direct incorporation of a stressful experience into dreams. In these last two examples, however, the incorporation occurred some nights after the test took place. I'll have more to say about the implications of this finding later on.

Therapy

Generally when we think of dreaming in relationship to therapy, we think of dream interpretation. We think of the dream being used as an instrument or adjunct to aid in the therapeutic process (see chapter 2). However, there have been a number of studies that were designed to explore the question of how therapy itself may specifically affect dreams and sleep.

In one such study,[14] Breger and his colleagues examined the effects of group therapy sessions on the dreams of the participants. During the course of therapy, each person in turn became the focus of the group for two sessions. Dreams were collected in the laboratory from each of the subjects both before and after they were the focus of the group. Basically, the findings showed that the focus sessions influenced dream content. Specifically, the issues discussed in the focus sessions appeared as the central themes of the dreams of the night. What is more, the researchers noted that the form of representation in the dream of these themes was specific to the individual dreamer.

In another study,[15] the dreams of patients undergoing psychotherapy were examined. The interesting thing about this study was that those people who were deemed to have had successful treatment had more anxiety connected with their dreams than did the patients whose treatment was judged to have been unsuccessful. The authors speculated that perhaps this was a function of the particular type of people they studied. That is, their subjects started out with particularly low levels of self-awareness and waking anxiety. Perhaps along with increased awareness as a function of therapy came an increase in waking anxiety, which in turn was reflected in an increase in anxiety in their dreams.

In one of our own studies,[16] we started out with a subject on the opposite end of the spectrum. The twenty-two year old man who volunteered for the study was beset by fears of noise and closed spaces. We decided to try to help our subject with a combination of relaxation training and desensitization. The therapy took place over a two week period. This enabled us to record nights of uninterrupted sleep as well as collect dreams before, during and after the treatment. We also asked our subject to write down any dreams he happened to remember on nights when he was not in the laboratory.

Shortly after treatment began, our subject had the following dream:

> I dreamed I was locked in a cage along with two other friends of mine. I can only remember one of the friends though, his name is J. and I've known him for about six years. The cage was made up of chicken wire and we were guarded by an animal. The animal was very big, like a bear, and kept on changing into other types of animals. This animal was actually another friend of mine transformed. His name is R. This animal kept on growling and snarling at us. Like I said there were three of us caged. Each of us had our own little cage inside the larger cage. The animal was attacking us in some part of the cage. I ran to my section and climbed up the wire. . . . The animal was right behind me. I was able to unlock the others as I ran past. We were all chased through the streets of crowds, until we came upon a house that seemed very familiar to me. The animal chased us up a flight of stairs, but when he came to the top he toppled over backwards and tumbled to his death. When we examined the dead body, it turned back into my friend R. We felt very bad, but were glad we had escaped. It was a very sunny, hot summer day.

The next dream occurred just as treatment was ending:

> I dreamed I was at some sort of beach. It was very warm and sunny out. The water was calm and a nice blue color. There were about six people there with me. I knew them in the dream but I don't know who they were now. The other people were lying on the sand very close to the water. I was swimming very close to the shore. The water wasn't shallow near the shore. . . . It got deep right away like a swimming pool. I called the others in for a swim but they wanted

to stay on the sand. I came out of the water and splashed them to try to get them into the water. Finally some of them came in. I was very relaxed, happy and content. Everything was warm and peaceful, and we had no troubles whatsoever. . . . either the dream ended there or I just can't remember any more.

These dreams are rather dramatic illustrations of how the content changed over the course of treatment. In the early dream, which is obviously highly charged with negative emotions, both claustrophobic and noise phobic elements are clearly represented. In the later dream, which is quite pleasant, these elements are not present. What is even more interesting, is that as the treatment progressed, our subject did still have dreams that contained both images of closed spaces and noise elements. However, they were no longer accompanied by fearful emotions. In other words, the dreams reflected the process and progress of the desensitization procedure. In the procedure, after learning relaxation techniques, the subject was asked to imagine the very events that frightened him. And just as was the case in his dreams, ultimately our subject was able to imagine those events while awake *without* any accompanying fear.

These results are similar to an anecdotal account of the treatment of a patient beset by conflicts of various kinds.[17] At the beginning of treatment, the patient reported that his dreams of these conflicts were aborted by anxiety-laden awakenings. As treatment progressed, he reported having the same type of dreams but without the accompanying anxiety and without the spontaneous awakenings.

Finally, a word about the uninterrupted recordings of sleep of our phobic subject. A couple of changes in his sleep patterns seemed to mirror his therapeutic progress and correspond to the changes we noted in our subject's dreams. Specifically, we found a decrease in time to sleep and a decrease in the number of REM period eye movements during the course of relaxation training. As we've noted earlier, these changes are consistent with a reduction in anxiety and dream emotionality respectively.

It is apparent from our discussion so far that presleep experiences can and do alter the content of our dreams. It also seems to be the case that the more dramatic those experiences are, the more likely it is that they will have an effect on both dream content and accompanying mood. However, there is one cautionary note. "Dramatic" or important is, as I mentioned earlier, in the eye of the beholder. A presleep event can only be considered stressful for an individual if that individual considers it to be stressful. For example, some years ago a student of mine set out to examine the effects of a stressful presleep experience on dreams.[18] As a stressor, he opted to use an extremely low-calorie diet. Diets of this type had previously been shown to be stressful. However, much to his surprise, his subjects did not find the diet stressful. Retrospectively, the reason for this seems rather obvious. The subjects in my student's study were obese women. Diets of one sort or another had become a way of life for these women. Indeed, many of their own, self-inflicted diets that they had tried at one time or another had been more stringent and onerous than the one my student used. So compared to those previous diets, the obese women found my student's diet to be a piece of cake (no pun intended).

Probably the most important lesson we can learn from the experience of my student is that ultimately what we dream is a reflection of a number of different things. Factors such as who we are, what circumstances we've encountered, and how we perceive the world around us all seem to play a role in the nature of our dreams. The who, what and how of our lives are in turn determined by a number of things ranging from the character of the society in which we live to our private idiosyncracies and the particular events that befall us.[19]

The section that follows is designed to provide a broad spectrum of examples of the various kinds of waking experiences that may find their way into dreams. It's a potpourri of studies and anecdotal accounts of different aspects of our waking lives that seem to have some relevance for the content of our dreams. It's by no means exhaustive.

VAGARIES OF OUR LIVES

There is probably no better way to start this section than with falling asleep. How do we do it, and what relationship does it have to the content of our dreams?

Falling Asleep

The other night, when I was having more than my usual difficulty working on this book, Jane and I were talking in bed. Just before I drifted off to sleep, I remember asking her if she'd read some of the manuscript. I was hoping she'd be able to make some suggestions to get me going again. That night I had the following dream: Jane was dressed in my shirt and my sweater. She was also wearing a hat of mine, of which I was particularly fond. I said to her, "While you're at it, why don't you write my book as well."

There is no mystery here. The book was very much on my mind. I wanted help with it. In the dream, the nature of the help went perhaps a little bit farther than what I would have dared to ask for in waking life. Nonetheless, I was without question asking for help just as I had as I drifted off to sleep.

My experience is very much like the events documented in a study that examined the relationship between the themes of subjects' dreams and their thoughts just prior to going to sleep.[20] In that study judges were able to successfully match the content of dreams with the content of the spontaneous thoughts of ten women just before they went to sleep in the laboratory.

If you think about it, these results are not all that surprising. Indeed, they seem quite consistent with the studies I've described earlier in this chapter. In most of those studies, subjects had some sort of presleep experience that they dreamed about during the course of the night. While we have no information about their thoughts just before they drifted off to sleep, it's not unreasonable to assume that when the presleep event was particularly potent, it would be on their minds when they went to sleep and consequently would appear in their dreams of the night.

The evidence we have from a couple of other studies[21] indicates that this is indeed the case. In those studies the authors presented the subjects with stressful and neutral films on different nights before they went to bed. In one of those studies they also used a suggestion session as a presleep stimulus. In the suggestion session, designed to heighten the intensity of the experimental situation, the experimenter suggested changes in the subjects' bodily sensations. The authors used an interesting technique to monitor the thoughts and images of their subjects as they drifted off to sleep. They placed halves of ping pong balls over the subjects' eyes and illuminated them with an even, red light. They also played monotonous white noise into the ears of the subjects. In effect they blotted out any of the normal external stimuli that impinge upon us when we fall asleep. Then they simply asked their subjects to start talking and to describe any thoughts, images or feelings they had. Subjects almost invariably drifted into a reverie* and then off to sleep as they spoke.

Perhaps not surprisingly, the themes and images of the reveries often reflected the presleep experiences of the subjects. And the themes and images of the reveries themselves in turn often found their way into the dreams

---

*This reverie that sometimes occurs on falling asleep is called a "hypnagogic reverie." One of the earliest systematic investigations of this phenomenon was reported by Silberer who used himself as his principal subject. (Silberer, H. (1951) Report on a method of eliciting and observing certain hallucination-phenomena. In D. Rapaport (Ed.) *Organization and pathology of thought*. New York: Columbia University Press.)

of the night. It's almost as if these reveries or our presleep thoughts act as conduits for some of what will ultimately appear in our dreams.

What happens then, on the way to sleep? Generally when we prepare to sleep, we seek out or try to create an unobtrusive environment. We darken the room. We shut the door to shut out sound. We may take the telephone off the hook. And so forth.

We also try to shut the door on our cares, our worries and our concerns. We try to turn off all forms of stimulation and excitement. Over the course of our lives each of us has probably devised special tricks of our own to provide ourselves with an innocuous psychological environment. Some of us count sheep. Others try to turn their minds into a blank. Still others may try to concentrate on pleasant yet mundane events. How successful we are probably depends on a lot of things. Noisy neighbors, a truck route past our front doors or a neon sign garishly shining through a torn curtain, may all make sleep difficult. So too, might stressful events of the day, or our anticipation of tomorrow's excitements and problems which we keep mulling over in our minds.

As we finally lose track of the environment around us, our ability to control our thoughts also seems to diminish.[22] Under these circumstances, it is not really startling that matters of importance will come surging back into our minds. Now, however, because we don't have the same facility to control our thought processes as we do when we are fully alert, these weighty concerns might swirl through our minds in a seemingly haphazard manner—in a manner somewhat similar to the way they might appear in dreams. So it seems reasonable to conceive of our thoughts and reveries before we go to sleep as a channel carrying material from our waking lives as fodder for our dreams.

Dream content thus seems ultimately to be a construction revolving around events in our lives as we understand them from our peculiar and particular perspectives. In the next section we'll consider how different perspectives of gender, age and changing circumstances may play a role in determining the nature of our dream content.

Gender and Changing Roles

Calvin Hall dubbed it a "ubiquitous sex difference in dreams."[23] Quite simply what he was referring to was the fact that "males dream more often of males than females do." This difference appears in literally thousands of dreams collected from an array of cultures by a number of different investigators under varying circumstances. For example, dreams have been collected from Mt. Everest climbers, United States · college students, Peruvian adolescents, the Zulu, the Hopi, Guatemalans and so forth. Of the thirty-five different groups and cultures from which dreams were obtained, twenty-nine of them exhibited this sex difference in their dreams.* How to explain this phenomenon?

In light of our discussion up to now, one obvious and simple explanation is that males may in fact be more important for males than females. That is males may simply spend more time and more significant time with males during their waking hours than they do with females and the ubiquity of males in their dreams merely reflects this ubiquity and importance in their waking lives.

Unfortunately, we have virtually no information about the waking relationships of the dreamers themselves in the studies I've just described. However, there is one study I know of which may indirectly shed some light on the problem. In that study,[24] dreams of working mothers were compared with those of homemakers. Among the differences in dream content which were found was the appearance of more male characters in the dreams of the working mothers than in the

---

*Of the remaining six groups, there were no instances when females dreamed more often of males than males did.

dreams of the mothers who stayed at home. Although here too we have no exact information about the amount of contact with males during the day, it is not unreasonable to assume that the working mothers were more likely to encounter males during their daily activities than the mothers who remained at home. This in turn would suggest that the dreams of the working mothers reflected their waking experience.

This view of the continuity between our waking and dreaming lives is also bolstered by a number of studies similar to the ones we just discussed. For example, Kramer and his colleagues[25] noted that changing roles of women seemingly altered some aspects of their dream content which previously differentiated them from men. Although, as in the previous studies I described, men in this study had more male characters in their dreams than women, there were no longer, among other things, differences between the sexes in the appearance of aggression in dreams. The authors speculated that the appearance of an equivalent amount of aggression in the dreams of both sexes, where formerly it had been predominantly the province of dreams of males, could be attributed to the "sexual revolution" and the concomitant changing roles of women in our society. The implications of this finding are clear. As the life of the individual changes the dream content changes in conjunction with it.

Indeed even studies of children's dreams[26] which demonstrated that dreams reflect the cognitive development of children are consistent with this notion. So too are the results from a study[27] of the emotional content of dreams of young and elderly women. The upper-middle class, elderly women enjoyed an apparently pleasant retirement. On the other hand, the younger women were in the first two years of college, uncertain and somewhat apprehensive as to what they were going to do in the future. The dreams of the latter group were more often characterized by the emotions of fear and anger, while the dreams of the former group were more often described as containing elements of enjoyment or joy.

The studies I have just described suggest that global life circumstances play a role in determining the content of our dreams. As we grow up, partly because of our cognitive development and partly because of the nature of our socialization, our life experiences and our understanding of those experiences are altered. These changes in the way we perceive the events in our waking lives in turn play a role in what forms the substance of our dreams and their accompanying emotions.

Gender and the consequent roles we assume as adults must surely have a profound impact on certain aspects of our dreams, but so too, do other life experiences that come our way, whether by design or chance. In the section that follows, I'll consider the impact of a few different types of life experiences on dreams. One thing these experiences have in common is that they are extremely important to the dreamer. Some of them are traumatic. The fact that such experiences appear in our dreams should be no surprise by now. Indeed in addition to the work we've discussed so far, there is a study that illustrates the importance of the emotionality of the waking experience in determining whether or not it ultimately finds its way into dream content.[28] In that study, it was found that the daytime activity accompanied by the most intense emotional tone was the one most likely to be represented in the dreams of the following night.

Some Profound Life Experiences

I want to start off this section with a couple of dreams two subjects had while they slept in my laboratory. I've always found these dreams to be particularly interesting for a number of reasons. First, they were obtained quite by chance. That is to say, the purpose of the study had nothing to do with dream content per se. The study involved multiple awakenings during the course of the night. In order to keep my subjects up for a short period of time after each awakening, I decided to have them report anything that happened to be going through their minds just prior to the awakening bell. Second, the subjects, again quite by chance, came to the laboratory at a time when important events in their lives had occurred or were in the process of unfolding. Each of them spoke about those particular events spontaneously and at great length. Third, on waking after having the dreams I'm about to describe, each of the subjects remarked on the dreams and wondered aloud about them. However, neither of them advanced any hypotheses as to the relationship of their dreams to their presleep experiences. I guess that leaves the task up to us.

The first subject arrived at the laboratory on a Wednesday evening. He was quite excited. The next day he was going directly from the laboratory to pick up a baby he and his wife had adopted. They had spent the entire day preparing a room for the new member of their family. It was their second adopted child. That night my subject reported a number of dreams that were focused in one way or another on the coming event. The first dream was obtained from an early REM period:

E: Was anything going through your mind before the bell rang?

S: Yes. We had taken the horses out to round up the cows. (Pause.) No! No! Scratch that. I know what it was. Er. Another fella and I were out collecting semen from this bull for artificial insemination. That's what it was.

E: Can you describe the scene and the other fellow in any more detail?

S: No just out on the farm . . . er . . . we were doing this in the pasture. The other fellow was along.

The second dream came later on in the night. Here is an excerpt from it:

E: Was anything going through your mind before the bell rang?

S: Well we were looking at some tricycles . . . er . . . It seems as if we were looking at some special kind of tricycle . . . maybe it was one of those tractor-pedal types.

E: You said we?

S: Yes, me and someone else were looking at tricycles, trying to find a particular one.[29]

In short, my subject's presleep preoccupation with an extremely important event in his life is clearly reflected in his dreams, albeit in a symbolic manner. It takes no quantum interpretative leap to recognize that the insemination dream is related in some manner to babies. Nor does it require any mental gymnastics to recognize that the tricycle dream is related to small children. And, of course, as we know, our subject's waking thoughts had centered around his bringing home the new baby.

While the dreams of the first subject reflected his anticipation of a joyous event in a symbolic manner, the dream of the next subject reflected a tragic event in a direct and undisguised fashion:

E: Was anything going through your mind before the bell rang?

S: Oh yeh. It just . . . I dreamt that I was, I was watching some people. They were all standing around in front of this church. It was, I think it was on a Sunday. And I remember everybody was all dressed up and everything. But there was this one man and I think what he did was, he was laying there on purpose but he was laying there between two, two cars, two parked cars by the side of the road and he had blood smeared all over him and his clothes were all torn up and everything and um . . . when the people came by, I think he was just laying there to see what their reactions were. And um . . . I can't remember if anybody asked him to come up to the church so that they could help him or if anybody asked if he was . . . um . . . hurt or anything. (Pause) I'm trying to think, like, let me think just a second. And he said . . . er . . . Oh! He asked them what kind of church this, it was, but they didn't say anything to him and that's all, that's all I can remember.

E: Were you in the dream?

S: I was just a spectator.[30]

This subject was an eighteen year old boy. He had come to the laboratory on the night following a funeral for his friend. His friend had been killed in a car accident a few days before and as you can well imagine the accident and death had been in the forefront of this teenager's thoughts. In fact, not surprisingly, he could talk of nothing else as we readied him for bed on this particular night. The bloodied man, the cars, the people going to church, the people not talking to (no longer able to talk to) the bloodied man are clear and straightforward representations in my subject's dream of his waking thoughts and experience.

Thus, the different yet profound events in the lives of these two young men, who happened to sleep in my laboratory in close proximity to the occurrence of those events, played a role in the content of their dreams. Of course there are many events that take place during our lives that may well have such a profound impact on us. Two such events, which happen to be related to one another, are getting married and getting divorced.

In 1930, Bagby[31] analyzed the dreams of a couple engaged to be married. He found that for both of them their inhibitions about sexual intercourse, intensified by their "flirtage," influenced the content of their dreams. He speculated this was often the case and even suggested that the examination of dreams of engaged couples would provide insight into how current emotional stress finds its way into dream content.

Similarly, a study[32] of the dreams of women in the midst of divorce revealed that divorce and the way they responded to it during waking life determined some of the characteristics of their dreams. Specifically, in this laboratory study, divorced women had a more negative tone in their dream reports gleaned from REM periods than a comparison group of married women who had never contemplated divorce. Not surprisingly, the divorcing women also dreamed about their roles as separated or ex-wives while no such references appeared in the dreams of the married women. So here again, we have an example of a potent life experience being represented directly in dreams.

Finally, we would be remiss if we didn't at least take note of the effect the ravages of war and political turmoil have on people and their ensuing dreams. While we have generally been aware of the effects these particular horrors have on waking experience, we are only now beginning to realize that they permeate every aspect of our lives, including our dreams. Indeed, we have already seen an example of how even the dreams of children of war victims may be influenced by the trauma of the war their parents experienced. In the case of Rosette (chapter 1) the mother's loss of a child during the holocaust had an impact on her relationship with Rosette, an impact which in turn found its way into Rosette's dream. Similarly, a number of Salvadoran refugees undergoing psychological assessment spontaneously complained of nightmares.[33] More than half reported they repeatedly dreamed of being pursued by men trying to kill them.

In addition, a number of studies of dreams of Vietnam veterans revealed that they too can be plagued by nightmares related to their wartime experiences. For example, in one study[34] it was reported that vivid nightmares of combat persisted eight to fifteen years after the war. Although therapy was able to ameliorate the sometimes nightly or weekly occurrences of these nightmares, they nevertheless would recur from time to time, apparently in response to other stressful waking experiences. In another study[35] self-reports of daydreams and sleep were obtained from Vietnam combat veterans and noncombatants. The daydreams of the combat veterans contained more elements of guilt and their sleep was more frequently punctuated by nightmares and characterized by insomnia than that of the noncombatants.

Finally, in still another study[36] the sleep of Vietnam combat veterans who were then currently experiencing regularly disturbing dreams was compared to that of other combatants who reported an absence of such dreams at the time of the study. The only difference between the sleep of these two groups was that the disturbed dreamers took a longer time to reach their first REM period. However, both groups exhibited a general pattern of sleep that differed dramatically from that of the normal population. For example, the veterans had more spontaneous awakenings during their sleep, spent more time awake and spent less time in REM sleep than the general population. Interestingly enough, all of the members of the group who were not currently experiencing disturbing dreams, had experienced them on a regular basis after finishing their service. Some of them still reported experiencing them from time to time, particularly when they were confronted by stressful events in their lives.

What these findings seem to suggest is simply that the effects of profoundly disturbing events may never go away. They undoubtedly intrude on our waking thoughts from time to time for the remainder of our lives. When they do, they no doubt find their way into our dreams as well. However, it's still an open question as to whether or not the apparent chronic change in sleep patterns will ever return to normal.

In this chapter we've explored the effects of different types of waking psychological experiences on dreams and sleep. We've discovered that, contrary to Freud's expectations, the more stressful events generally have a greater impact on our sleeping lives than neutral or benign ones. These findings are ubiquitous. They occur with a wide variety of presleep experiences.

It also seems unlikely that such presleep experiences gain entry into our dreams only insofar as they hook up with unfulfilled wishes (chapter 2). Rather, it seems more likely that emotionally laden waking experiences are able to direct or alter the content of dreams which as we have seen are a regular and inexorable part of the sleep cycle. Or to put it another way, there seems to be some sort of continuity between our waking experiences and the nature of our dreams.

In the next chapter we'll examine how changes in our bodies may also alter our sleep and dreams.

6

Our Bodies, Our Dreams

While Freud gave little credence to the idea that daytime events could be instigators of dreams, he clearly felt that internal, somatic events could cause dreams. However, as we've already mentioned, since dreams are a regularly occurring part of the sleep cycle, the notion that they can be caused by any sort of chance event including bodily disturbances seems to be a highly unlikely one. This doesn't mean somatic events can't alter ongoing dreams. For example, the other night I was dreaming about a person with whom I'm acquainted, who at times can be very unpleasant to his children.* In the dream, he became abusive towards me and then tied a rope around my wrist. He drew the rope tighter and tighter and it became quite painful. I suddenly awoke to discover I had been lying on my hand which was in a twisted position. I was in fact in some pain. Evidently, the pain of my twisted limb had been incorporated into the ongoing dream about this unpleasant man.

In the sections that follow, I'll describe some studies that were designed to explore if and how various types of

---

*Not surprisingly Jane and I had been talking about this fellow at dinner earlier in the evening—yet another example of presleep events finding their way into dreams (chapter 5).

somatic events may affect both sleep patterns and the nature of dreams.

THIRST

Earlier (chapter 2), I described one of Freud's dreams of "convenience." He had dreams of this nature with some frequency after eating salty food before going to bed. He felt this particular dream was induced by a developing thirst. In general, he believed dreams of convenience are attempts to satisfy a need in order to protect the dreamer from being awakened by a disturbing stimulus. By using laboratory techniques, it became possible to systematically explore the specific effects of thirst on both sleep and dreams.

In one of our own studies,[1] we deprived subjects of food and water for a twenty-four hour period.* When they arrived at the laboratory for the experimental night, we asked them to indicate how thirsty they were on a scale that ranged from "not thirsty at all" to "extremely thirsty."** Then we wired them up and for good measure gave them a little bedtime snack of salty crackers. Finally, we allowed them to go to sleep.

One of our subjects reported the following dream on his first REM period awakening:

> Yeh. Okay. Well I remember I was sitting up in or was it. No, it was some, no, it was up in my room and we had some beer up there. We—I think we had about . . . well we had some cold ones and some warm ones, anyway and I didn't want to open up my warm one. I was going to drink this other guy's cold one and he

---

*The subjects slept in our laboratory for a night and then were accompanied throughout the day by an experimenter to make sure they didn't eat, drink or take a nap.

**Needless to say all our subjects indicated they were thirsty.

kinda, kind of didn't like that, that was our discussion before, I guess it must have been one or two minutes or so. It seems like . . . in dream time. But, and then, oh, and then after I took one last swallow of beer and it wasn't good 'cos it was all foamy so I spit it in the sink (laugh). That's all I remember.

On a subsequent awakening, the same subject had the following dream:

Just as you rang the bell and you were, and you were getting a drink of water but this, but this time you gave me a, um, well some ice to put in it, but it looked like an ashtray, and I broke it in pieces and dropped it in the glass but you wouldn't give me any water and you gave this other guy some water.

In both of these dreams, the themes reflect the concerns of the water-deprived dreamer. In both cases, he was prevented from alleviating his thirst. In the first case, it was because the beer was foamy and didn't taste good. The second dream was a more direct representation of the dreamer's situation. He was trying to slake his thirst, but I was preventing him from doing so.

In the following dream, of another subject, the dreamer was also frustrated from slaking his thirst. This time it was because the champagne changed to juice which in turn changed to soup!

I'd woken up and I was home again. I was rummaging through the refrigerator looking for something to eat. And er, I went through all sorts of stuff. There was a quarter of a bottle of champagne in the fridge. Only er, I looked closer, it looked like it was orange juice in it. And then as I got it out I noticed somebody had put soup in there.

One final example from still another subject. It's almost like "The Rime of the Ancient Mariner" with water everywhere:

Let's see. Oh, this time I was in the, oh yeah, I was in the water, sort of ice water, sort of fooling around. And my girlfriend was there and one guy was there and we were sort of splashing each other. And er, the ice was just breaking up off the water and it was . . . it must have been quite cold but it didn't bother us then. And, er . . . so we were . . . pushing chunks of ice around and splashing water on each other. I don't know for sure if there was actually someone else there beside me and my girlfriend. There might have been one other guy. But I remember quite clearly how the, I was watching the ice float on the water. Pushing the ice along. Water looked nice and clear and cold. I think that's about all for that one.

All of these dreams then, with their central themes of thirst or water, reflected the circumstances of the dreamers who had been deprived of water for twenty-four hours. But just as we've seen with the dreams of our film-study subjects (chapter 5), the same circumstance gave rise to characteristically different dreams for each of the dreamers. The first two dreamers were being frustrated in their attempts to slake their thirst. In fact, for one of them, I am obviously correctly identified as the source of the frustration. The last dreamer, however, seemed to be quite satisfied to play about in the water. Interestingly, in none of these dreams is the dreamer ever actually able to slake his thirst.

In another study,[2] it was also found that day-long water deprivation altered dream content. The subjects were provided with a rather fancy, spicy, thirst-producing spaghetti dinner before they went to sleep. In that study, some of the subjects had dreams in which they were slaking their thirst, very much like the dreams of convenience Freud described.

Just as was the case with the stressful films, there is evidence that water deprivation can also influence the pattern of uninterrupted sleep. For example, in a study designed to explore the effects of thirst on the sleep cycle,[3] subjects spent one night in the laboratory when they had not undergone water deprivation and another night after they had been without water for twenty-two hours. Just before going to bed on the latter night, they were treated to our usual salty cracker diet.

After water deprivation, the subjects spent less time in REM periods and had more body movements throughout the night than when they were not deprived of water. Here again, we see that a stimulus that affected the content of dreams also had the capacity to alter at least some aspects of sleep as well.

EXERCISE

Exercise seems to be the "in thing" to do these days. Every time I turn around it seems to me a new fitness palace has emerged. Practically everyone I know is singing the praises of jogging, aerobics, swimming, body building, tennis, bike riding, skiing or just plain walking *briskly*. It seems to me I can't go to a party these days without someone insisting on telling me how far they've jogged or how long they "rode" on their stationary bikes that day.

Most of us believe all this frantic activity has some beneficial effect for us and for our bodies. Some of us believe physical exercise helps us sleep better. As it turns out, it's difficult to make any blanket statement about the effect of exercise on sleep. Comparing the results of the many studies in this area is somewhat like comparing apples to oranges. This is because different studies have used subjects with varying degrees of physical prowess. They have also explored a diverse spectrum of physical activities. In addition, in some cases the exercises have been performed just before going to bed and in others at some point earlier in the day.

In spite of this difficulty let's take a look at a few of the studies that have tried to examine the effects of exercise on sleep. Their results may at least lead us to some interesting speculations. I also want to tell you about the one study I know of that attempted to explore the effects of exercise on dream content. It had some interesting results.

In one study,[4] subjects who were described as people who tended to be "slightly above average in daily physical exertion," were required to squeeze a hand dynamometer for two periods of forty minutes, two hours before they went to bed. After doing the exercise, these subjects fell asleep more quickly, had more slow wave sleep* and had fewer body movements during their first sleep cycle than when they had no presleep exercise.

In another study,[5] normally "active" subjects and normally "non-active" subjects performed a highly intense exercise which lasted for between twenty-five and thirty minutes. They did the exercise at about four o'clock in the afternoon and went to bed at their normal bedtimes. For all of the subjects there was an elevation in sleeping heart rate for the first two hours of sleep and a reduction in the length of the first REM period. However, the active subjects displayed an increase in slow wave sleep and an increased length of time to reach a REM period during the first cycle, while the non-active subjects had less slow wave sleep and reached their first REM period more quickly.

In still another study,[6] the sleep of runners capable of running a marathon was examined after a day of rest, after a day of training and for two successive nights after competing in a race. There was no change in slow wave sleep for these well-conditioned athletes after the race. However, after the race they did have a heightened heart rate at night and took a longer time to reach their first REM period than either after the day of rest or after the training day.

---

*Slow wave sleep is comprised of stages 3 and 4 (chapter 3).

Finally, Hauri[7] compared the sleep patterns at the beginning of the night of subjects who spent six hours relaxing, six hours doing strenuous physical activity or six hours involved in intensive mental work. Later in the night, after they had accumulated at least three and a half hours of sleep, he awakened the subjects and collected their dreams.[8] As we might expect, Hauri found that heart and respiratory rate was greatest on falling asleep after the exercise session. What was perhaps most surprising was it took his subjects longer to fall asleep after the mental activity than after either the relaxation period or the physical activity.

There are a number of interesting facets about these studies when we examine them together. First, it seems clear that all people who engage in strenuous physical exercise, whether right before bedtime or earlier in the day, have a higher heart rate on reaching sleep than they would if they had not engaged in such an activity. However, intense mental work may be more likely to delay the onset of sleep than strenuous physical effort. And finally, the general pattern of sleep seems to be altered as a function of strenuous exercise. For the "relatively" active person the alteration seems to be manifested by an increase in the length of the first sleep cycle, that is, an increase in the length of time until the first REM period. However, for the "non-active" subjects the first sleep cycle is somewhat shortened. The reasons these types of changes occur are still a subject of controversy. But nonetheless they do occur. And it will probably come as no surprise to you by now that these changes in the sleep cycle are accompanied by alterations in dream content. What may be a surprise though is the nature of the dream content changes. They are not exactly what you might well have come to expect.

In the study[9] I mentioned before, in which dreams were collected on the nights following either strenuous physical exercise or intense mental work, subjects tended to dream *less* about the activity they had engaged in for the six hours prior to sleep. So, for example, after physical exercise, subjects were more likely to dream about sitting around or reading. Similarly, after studying, there was less dream content related to thinking or problem-solving than after either the six hours of physical exercise or the six hours of relaxation.

What is particularly important about this finding is that it is often cited as evidence for what has come to be known as the "compensatory" notion of the function of dreams. Briefly, the compensatory notion suggests that dream life may be complementary to waking life. In this view, one of the functions of dreams may be to supply the dreamer with activities or emotions that are lacking in his or her waking life. I'll discuss this notion and other contemporary theories of dream function at greater length later on.

SLEEPING PILLS AND ALCOHOL

So here we are. We're very into exercise and fitness. We want to ban pollutants from the environment and additives and pesticides from our food. Yet at the same time, many of us pop pills and consume alcohol at an ever increasing rate. Often we take these pills or have a drink or two or three before going to bed because we want to have a "good night's sleep." Well exactly what effects do these substances have on our sleep and dreams? Do they in fact provide us with a good night's sleep and sweet dreams?

In the case of sleeping pills, as with exercise, it's difficult to make any blanket statements on the issue. This is because there are a vast number of drugs on the market. Not only do they vary in their general effects on sleep and dream content, but their effects may also vary as a function of dosage, symptomatology and the like. However, it is clear that almost all sleeping pills alter the sleep cycle to some extent. Most of them result in a reduction in the amount of time spent in REM sleep and a reduction in the eye movements associated with the REM sleep that remains.

It is also clear that sleeping pills can alter the content of dreams. For example, in one study,[10] it was found that barbiturates caused dreams to be more conceptual and thoughtlike than they were normally. However, the more powerful impact may come when the medication is withdrawn. Such withdrawal effects were documented in a study of the effects of hypnotics on sleep patterns, dreaming and mood state.[11] It was found that not only did REM sleep occur in abnormally high amounts* when the use of the drugs was discontinued but the nature of the dreams was altered as well. Following withdrawal, the dreams of the subjects became more intense and unpleasant and several of them were classified as nightmares.

Interestingly enough, some of the same effects I've just described can be found with the self-prescribed, over-the-counter drug called alcohol. However, the difference is that alcohol doesn't even seem to guarantee you an uninterrupted night's sleep. Having several large drinks before going to bed may indeed enable you to fall asleep. But more often than not, you will awaken in the middle of the night and have difficulty going back to sleep. Indeed, the pattern of sleep of alcoholics often involves heavy drinking before going to bed, followed by a repeat of the dosage on awakening in the middle of the night to enable them to return to sleep.[12] In fact, a study of the effects of alcohol on the sleep pattern of normal subjects revealed that large doses of alcohol increased sleep disturbances in the latter part of the night.[13] This study as well as another one[14] also showed that alcohol, just like sleeping pills, reduces the amount of time spent in REM sleep.

The effects of alcohol on sleep mimic those of sleeping pills in another respect. Withdrawal from alcohol can result in a profound REM rebound effect.[15]

To my knowledge, there are no studies of the effects of alcohol on dreaming in a non-alcoholic population. However, studies of dreams of alcoholics do suggest that

---

*A reduction in the amount of the usual time spent in REM sleep often results in an increase in REM time on subsequent night(s). This is referred to as "REM rebound."

drinking alters dream content both during ingestion and at the time of withdrawal, again as was the case with sleeping pills. The nature of these changes in dream content seems to vary from individual to individual.[16] For example, after drinking alcohol some subjects dreamed of traumatic episodes, while others experienced an increase in emotionality in their dreams on withdrawal.

In sum then, it's safe to say that stimuli such as alcohol, sleeping pills, exercise and the like all have the potential to alter both dream content and the sleep cycle. For want of a better term, these types of somatic stimuli might be designated as externally induced. That is, they are stimuli that we choose to "inflict" on our bodies. While they are somatic stimuli, they are stimuli over which we have some degree of control. However, there are other types of spontaneously occurring somatic stimuli over which we have little or no control. These are internally induced stimuli. The next couple of sections are concerned with these types of somatic stimuli.

THE MENSTRUAL CYCLE

Studying the effects of the menstrual cycle on the emotionality of dreams turned out to be an intriguing proposition. There was certainly the commonly held belief that menses is a stressful waking experience. Consequently, we started out by expecting to find that menses would alter the emotion of dreams much as any other stressful experience.

We began by examining the literature on the effects of the menstrual cycle on the waking state. Much to our surprise, the results of the research from a number of studies were inconsistent. They indicated the effects of the menstrual cycle on the waking state ranged from no change in mood[17] to far-reaching disturbances in both performance and mood,[18] and included everything in between.

There was similar disagreement on the effect of the menstrual cycle on sleep itself and on dream recall. For example, one study[19] found changes in the amount of

REM time at the end of the night late in the menstrual cycle. Another study[20] found changes only in non-REM sleep. Garfield[21] found the smallest number of dreams were recalled premenstrually and the most at midcycle while Trinder and his colleagues[22] reported no significant changes in dream recall as a function of the menstrual cycle.

Maybe these different results were akin to what happened in the case of the blind men and the elephant. If you recall, in the poem by John Saxe, six blind men went to see an elephant. Each touched different parts of the beast, and as a consequence each had an entirely different conception of what an elephant looked like. In a similar manner, perhaps the different women who participated in these various studies experienced differing amounts of distress in the course of their menstrual cycles, distress which could ultimately affect their waking lives as well as their sleep.

To guard against the effects of these types of individual differences, we[23] screened potential subjects using a Menstrual Distress Questionnaire. We chose those women who had low levels of self-rated menstrual distress to participate in our study. Ten women slept in our laboratory for a total of five nights. Dreams were collected from a premenstrual night, a menstrual night and a midcycle night. We found no differences in waking mood, dreaming mood or dream recall as a function of the time of the menstrual cycle.

However, in another study,[24] this one involving the collection of dreams in a diary at home, women who showed an increase in waking premenstrual and menstrual stress also exhibited an increase in anxiety and hostility in their dreams. The findings of this study, taken together with those of our own, would seem to corroborate the idea that the potential for the menstrual cycle to disturb dream content is a function of its particular effects on the individual woman. This is not unlike some of the studies we examined earlier demonstrating differences between people in the degree and nature of their responses during sleep and dreaming to waking stimuli that are apparently the same (chapter 5).

ILLNESS

At one time or another during the course of our lives, all of us suffer from various types of illnesses. They can range from the simple cold to chronic diseases to illnesses requiring major intervention such as surgery. Up to now, we have been discussing how somatic conditions are reflected in our dreams or in our sleep. In respect to physical illness, the same question may be asked. Do physical ailments alter dream content? Or to put it another way, are physical ailments somehow reflected in our dreams? However, in the case of physical ailments there is an additional problem that crops up. Is it the stress of *knowing* that you have an ailment rather than the somatic effects of the ailment that alters the dream content?

For example, in a study[25] of dreams of patients about to undergo major surgery, it was found the upcoming surgery was often prominently featured in their dream content. Each of the five subjects studied had different ailments and different somatic symptoms. But it was the fact of having an ailment that required surgery, rather than the ailment itself, that seemed to be responsible for the greatest alteration in the content of the dreams of these patients.

Nonetheless, there are some studies and clinical case histories that suggest that dreams can reflect the somatic condition itself. For example, in one clinical report[26] a patient had a dream in which she was hanging by a window ledge and, ultimately weakened, fell to the ground. Some days later she fainted and was found to be suffering from a chronic infection of the bladder. In this case, the dream apparently reflected a somatic condition that was affecting the patient, even though she was not consciously aware of it.

In a retrospective study[27] of patients with a number of different severe medical problems, a relationship was found between some aspects of dream content and clinical outcomes. In men, dream references to death, and in women, dream references to separation, were related to poor clinical outcomes. Similarly, in another study,[28] the severity of cardiac patients' disease at the time of assessment was reflected in the nature of their dreams. As in the previous study, references to death in the dreams of men and separation in the dreams of women were related to the severity of the cardiac dysfunction. In these two studies, then, all the patients were aware they had a severe malady, although they evidently were not consciously aware of the degree of severity of their illness. However, it was precisely the severity of their illness that seemed to be responsible for the alteration of the dream content.

Up to now we've considered some of the possible effects illness or knowledge of illness may have on dream content. However, there is another interesting, related question which is worth looking at. Can dreams affect the course of an illness? Or at least can dreams induce somatic symptoms of an illness? This question has come up specifically in reference to so-called psychosomatic diseases. Such illnesses are typified during the waking state by somatic responses to stressful events. Two such illnesses are ulcers and asthma.

To examine the effects of dreams on these diseases is no simple matter. The best we can do is let people with a psychosomatic illness sleep through the night and map any somatic disturbances that may occur. If such disturbances occur during REM sleep, we can at least speculate that it was the REM-period dream content that resulted in the disturbance.

For example, in one study[29] the acid secretion of a group of hospitalized duodenal ulcer patients was compared with that of a group of patients hospitalized for other maladies. In general, we know that during the waking state gastric acid secretion increases at times of stress. During the course of the night, the ulcer patients exhibited a variation in the amount of gastric acid secretion, with the greatest amount occurring during REM sleep. The non-ulcer patients, on the other hand, exhibited little variation in the amount of acid secretion during the course of the night. These results were interpreted as indicating that psychologically distressing dreams were responsible for the increase in REM-period gastric discharges in the ulcer patients.

All night sleep recordings of patients with asthma, as well as some dream reports of asthmatic patients, obtained during the course of psychotherapy, raised the possibility that dreams can also induce asthmatic episodes. Hartmann[30] reported a study in which twenty-one of thirty-nine nocturnal asthmatic attacks occurred during REM sleep. As he pointed out, this is a far greater proportion occurring during REM sleep than one would expect by chance. He interpreted these results as indicating that dreaming sleep may have been stressful and consequently resulted in the onset of somatic symptoms in his asthmatic patients. As a counterpoint to this study, reports[31] from psychotherapy that nocturnal asthmatic episodes were often accompanied by nightmares with themes of strangulation or drowning are extremely interesting.

Of course these results can just as easily be interpreted as dreams reflecting a somatic state rather than causing a somatic response. It is really a chicken or egg question. But one thing does seem to be certain when we take all of these studies together. There is an interrelationship between dream content and the state of our bodies. Whether this interrelationship occurs directly during sleep or is a result of the waking thoughts we take to bed with us is still not clear.

Certainly, as we saw in the last chapter, stressful waking thoughts can and do influence dream content. Hence it is not surprising that involvement with and thoughts about an illness during wakefulness can play a role in the nature of subsequent dream content. I can think of no better illustration of this than Audrey Foy's notes on dreams she obtained from *both* patients and staff on a dialysis unit of the New York Veterans Administration Hospital.[32] As she pointed out, the patients and staff shared the same concerns albeit from different prospectives. To the patient it was concern for his or her own life. For the staff member it was the feeling of grave responsibility for the lives of the patients. As a consequence of these shared waking anxieties and stressful experiences, patients and staff alike shared a spectrum of dream themes reflecting those mutual concerns.

7

Things That Go Bump in the Night

Even on the surface of it, the relationship we have with our environment while we sleep seems to be a rather peculiar one. There are plenty of anecdotal accounts of parents sleeping blissfully through intensely loud thunderstorms, yet awakening at the single muted cry of their baby in the next room.

Last summer, when I was returning home after a long walk in the park, one of our neighbors said to me, "That was some accident last night." It was only then that I noticed bits and pieces of glass and metal strewn on the boulevard. As it turned out the accident had occurred right in front of my house at about three o'clock in the morning. A car driven at high speed had careened into a parked car, bounced off a tree and overturned on the boulevard. Fortunately no one was seriously hurt, but the noise from the impact was so great it awakened many people. In fact, I found out a couple of days later that a friend of mine and his family who live more than a block away had been awakened by the noise and had gone to the scene of the accident. Yet, although our bedroom windows front onto the boulevard where the accident occurred, Jane and I slept through the accident as well as the aftermath, including the arrival of the police and an ambulance!

Why were we able to sleep through this incredible racket which awakened others more than a block away? How can parents sleep through the crash of a thunderstorm yet be awakened by the tiny cries of their infant? These are not simple questions, nor as we shall see do they have any simple answers.

Let's dispense with the obvious first. There are no doubt times when our hypothetical parents are awakened by even one loud clap of thunder. There are surely also times when they aren't awakened by their baby's cries until they become louder and more insistent. But we are still left with the basic question of how and why we respond to some of the stimuli that confront us and not to others when we are asleep. Obviously, it is not just a question of how loud or intense the stimulus may be.

Apparently if a stimulus is intense enough to be registered at the level of the cortex in the brain while we sleep, we are capable of making some sort of decision about its relevance or importance to us. However, the decision-making process may not always be a straightforward one. For example, it is quite possible that if we are dreaming at the time of the stimulation we might ignore the stimulus because we are attending to the dream. Another possibility is we might understand the stimulus in the context of the ongoing dream, that is, incorporate the stimulus into the dream, in a manner that robs it of its significance for us.

Some lovely examples of this can be found in Hildebrandt's alarm clock dreams that Freud reported. Let's take a look at two of them.

> I dreamt, then, that one spring morning I was going for a walk and was strolling through the green fields till I came to a neighbouring village, where I saw the villagers in their best clothes, with hymn-books under their arms, flocking to the church. Of course! It was Sunday, and early morning service would soon be beginning. I decided I would attend it; but first, as I

was rather hot from walking, I went into the church-yard which surrounded the church, to cool down. While I was reading some of the tombstones, I heard the bellringer climbing up the church tower and at the top of it I now saw the village bell which would presently give the signal for the beginning of devotions. For quite a while it hung there motionless, then it began to swing, and suddenly its peal began to ring out clear and piercing—so clear and piercing that it put an end to my sleep. But what was ringing was the alarm-clock.

In the second dream:

It was a bright winter's day and the streets were covered with deep snow. I had agreed to join a party for a sleigh-ride; but I had to wait a long time before news came that the sleigh was at the door. Now followed the preparations for getting in—the fur rug spread out, the foot-muff put ready—and at last I was sitting in my seat. But even then the moment of departure was delayed until a pull at the reins gave the waiting horses the signal. Then off they started, and, with a violent shake, the sleigh bells broke into their familiar jingle—with such violence, in fact, that in a moment the cobweb of my dream was torn through. And once again it was only the shrill sound of the alarm-clock.[1]

Freud suggested that Hildebrandt's dreams were initiated by his alarm clock ringing while he slept; that he had formed "illusions" around a stimulus not yet clearly perceived. The illusions or dreams in turn served to protect his sleep. But as we've already noted, the fact that dreams are a regularly occurring part of the sleep cycle would make it extremely unlikely that they could be instigated by random events. This obviously would be as true for events occurring in the environment around us while we sleep as it is for internal, somatic stimuli (chapter 6). What is more likely is that the sound of the alarm clock ringing was woven into the fabric of already ongoing dreams.

This is not to say that the ringing may not have altered the content of Hildebrandt's dreams. Quite the contrary. It is quite possible that if the alarm clock had not sounded, Hildebrandt would have not dreamed of either church bells or sleigh bells ringing. Perhaps his dreams would have taken an entirely different tack.

Now let's carry our speculation a little further. In the first dream, the presence of the belfry and the bellringer were compatible with the ringing sound of the alarm clock. In the second dream, the existence of a sleigh with its bells also was consistent with the ringing alarm clock. So in these two dreams, the particular stimulus was capable of being understood by Hildebrandt in a manner consistent with the dream narrative. As a result, he was able to continue sleeping. In this sense, it may be reasonable to consider dreams as the "guardians" of sleep. However, when the stimulus persisted, its real origin could no longer be misconstrued and Hildebrandt was awakened.

But what if Hildebrandt was having a dream inconsistent with ringing bells. Let's say, for example, he was dreaming that he was drifting in the middle of the ocean. Under those circumstances, we might speculate, the sound of his alarm clock could not be misinterpreted. Its jarring noise would presumably have awakened him immediately.

All of this is by way of saying our relationship to our environment while we sleep is a rather complicated one. The form and intensity of external stimuli, their importance to us, and whether or not we are dreaming at the time they occur all probably play a role in determining whether or not, and how, we respond to them.

ENVIRONMENTAL EFFECTS ON DREAM CONTENT

Among the earliest investigations of the effects of external events on dream content were those conducted by Maury[2] in the middle of the nineteenth century. Maury had an assistant do a number of different things to him while he slept. Although not all of the experiments were successful, some of the stimuli affected the content of Maury's dreams. For example, when he was tickled on the nose with a feather, he dreamed of being tortured. In the dream a mask was placed on Maury's face and then pulled off taking the skin with it. When he was pinched on the neck, Maury dreamed of getting a mustard plaster put on him. When water was placed on his forehead, he dreamed he was in Italy, sweating heavily and drinking white wine. When candle light was shone on him through a sheet of red paper, Maury dreamed of heat. And so forth.

In a similar type of study, Cubberly[3] placed sticky paper on different parts of his body before going to sleep. He concluded that most of the time he either dreamed of the specific parts of his body that had the adhesive on it or else dreamed of tensions which he attributed to the sticky material.

With the discovery of the sleep cycle and the relationship of dreaming to REM sleep, it became possible to examine the effects of external stimulation on dream content in a more systematic fashion. Dement and Wolpert[4] set about to do just that by presenting their subjects with various stimuli during REM sleep. They used a tone, a light and a spray of water as their stimuli. They found that the water spray was most readily incorporated into dreams (a little more than forty percent of the time) while the tone was least likely to appear in their subjects' dreams (about nine percent of the time). However, Berger[5] found a much higher incidence of incorporation (more than fifty percent of the time) when he used either meaningful or nonmeaningful names as stimuli during REM periods.

How could we account for this discrepancy in the amount of incorporation of the two auditory stimuli? There were several possibilities. One had to do with the nature of the stimuli themselves. Perhaps names, because they are intrinsically more meaningful than tones, are more readily incorporated into dreams. Another possibility was that the discrepancy in the results was due to the more sensitive measures of incorporation used in the second study. But still another and perhaps the most intriguing possibility had to do with a procedural difference between the two studies. In order to insure that the subjects actually heard the names, Berger had played them over a loud speaker until there were slight changes in the EEG. Dement and Wolpert had done no such thing. Could Berger's names have awakened the subjects, albeit momentarily? Was it possible that at least some of the time Dement and Wolpert's subjects never even heard the tone?

Fortunately for me, just about the time I became aware of this problem, Bill Goff and Truett Allison, who were then at Yale University, came up with a way around it. They had devised a technique of stimulation that was certain to reach the level of the cortex of sleeping subjects without awakening them. This meant that it would be possible to explore some of the effects of the environment on our dreams without worrying about whether the stimulus had been registered by the subjects and without running the risk of awakening them.

The technique, which I mentioned in chapter 3, involved giving the subjects painless shocks to the wrist. Don't cringe! I can assure you the shocks were indeed painless. Like all sleep researchers using a new technique, I tried the procedure out on myself before daring to subject anyone else to it. I am by nature easily as cowardly as the next person and particularly afraid of electricity, but I spent a day in a laboratory at Yale, learning the technique and experiencing the shocks many times over until I was convinced that they were both harmless and painless.

What Goff and Allison had discovered was that shocks given to the median nerve at the wrist at an intensity high enough to make the thumb move during the waking state, would be certain to be registered at the cortex when the person was asleep. The plan of my study[6] was quite straightforward. Subjects were wired for sleep recording and both wrists were hooked up to the stimulating apparatus. During REM periods in a predetermined random fashion, I stimulated either their right or left wrist or else I didn't give them any stimulation.* The stimulation was presented either at the beginning of the REM period or after the REM period had been going on for three minutes. The ten male subjects were awakened at varying times after the stimulation and were asked to relate anything going through their minds directly before the awakening buzzer. Finally, the content of their dreams was assessed by a judge who had no knowledge of the conditions under which the dreams were obtained. She analyzed them according to a number of different criteria, including whether there was direct, indirect or no representation of the stimulus in the dreams. In chapter 3, I described a couple of dreams in which the stimulus was directly represented. Here is another one:

> . . . The thought was I felt a pinch in my hand. Electrical impulse. With this electrical impulse I was awake and I got up outa bed and I sat near a desk. I looked at the time and it was five o'clock and I went back to bed again. And the phone rang and I realized it was just a dream. . . .[7]

Overall, I found that the stimulus was incorporated into the subjects' dreams about fifty-six percent of the

---

*Subjects did not know on which wrist or indeed *if* they would be stimulated prior to a particular awakening.

time.* But there were a couple of other aspects of the results that are particularly interesting.

For one thing, each of the subjects tended to respond to the stimulus presentations in his own characteristic manner most of the time. For example, one of my subjects had a number of stimulated dreams in which he dreamed that someone he was trying to ignore was tugging at his sleeve. During the postsleep interview, he made the connection between the sleeve-tugging episodes and the stimulation. Another subject had several dreams during stimulation in which he was wired up and his thumb was moving just as it might during the waking state. While for still another subject, the appearance of the stimulus in the dream was rarely apparent. In short, as we have seen in relation to presleep and somatic stimulation, there were individual variations in the way the dreamer went about dealing with environmental instrusions while asleep. Some people appeared more likely to ignore it, while others appeared more likely to weave it into an existing dream.

The other facet of this study I found fascinating concerned changes in dream content other than incorporation of the electrical stimulation. In addition to examining whether or not the stimuli were incorporated into the dreams, I also looked at whether the structure of the dreams was somehow altered by the stimuli. In particular, I was interested to see whether or not the fact that I was stimulating the body of the dreamer would increase the importance of the dreamer's body in the dream as well as

---

*By chance, there were nine instances when the EEG record indicated very brief periods of awakening during the stimulation. While the dreams obtained from these REM periods were not included in the main analysis, I examined them for incorporation of the stimulus anyway. Seven of these nine dreams (or seventy-eight percent) exhibited some degree of incorporation. So apparently, transient awakenings do aid in incorporation of external events.

his bodily activity. What I found was that rather than the dreamer's body being more important and active in the dreams, the bodies of other people in the dream became more important and more active. This finding is also consistent with Freud's notion of dreams being the guardians of sleep. In respect to external stimuli, he wrote, "Either the mind pays no attention at all to occasions for sensation during sleep—if it is able to do this despite the intensity of the stimuli and the significance which it knows it attaches to them; or it makes use of a dream in order to deny the stimuli; or, thirdly, if it is obliged to recognize them, it seeks for an interpretation of them which will make the currently active sensation into a component part of a situation which is wished for and which is consistent with sleeping. The currently active sensation is woven into the dream *in order to rob it of reality.*"[8] Thus, one might speculate that by transferring the increased bodily activity to the other in the dream, the stimulus was robbed of some of its significance to the dreamer which in turn permitted him to continue sleeping.

Interestingly enough, similar results were obtained in another study with a different type of stimulus.[9] In that study, the subjects were instructed to turn off a tone played while they were asleep by taking a deep breath. Whether or not the subjects were able to respond,* they were awakened after the tone had ended.

It was found that if the subjects had been dreaming, they were less likely to either respond to the tone in the prescribed manner or be awakened by it than if they had not been dreaming. But particularly striking was the finding that subjects were even more unlikely to either respond to the tone or be awakened by it when the meaning of the tone was altered in the dream. For example, in one dream a subject reported being on "Fantasy Island"

---

*If the subject didn't respond the tone was terminated after sixteen seconds.

where a bell was ringing in an attempt to get people to come together. In this instance, she did not respond to the stimulus. However, a subject who reported dreaming of a high pitched tone which was making her cry did turn off the tone by taking a deep breath. So here again, in the first example we have an instance of an external stimulus being woven into a dream context that is consistent with the dreamer remaining asleep. The stimulus is in essence robbed of its significance to the dreamer.

But what of stimuli occurring during sleep that are intrinsically significant to the dreamer during his or her waking life? Would they be more likely to have an impact on dreams than less important stimuli? And what might the nature of that impact be?

In one study,[10] subjects were asked to write a brief description of their ten major concerns and then pick a couple of words that identified each of those concerns. They were also asked to pick a couple of words that they associated with issues that were of concern to others but not to themselves. After the subjects went to sleep, either the concern-related or nonconcern-related words were played to them while they slept. After the stimulation, the subjects were awakened and dreams were collected. As we might expect, the concern-related words were more frequently incorporated into REM-period dreams than the nonconcern-related words. These results suggest that, at least during REM periods, we are not only aware of stimuli in the environment but we respond to them differently as a function of their meaning to us.

In a study of our own,[11] Joseph De Koninck and I examined what effect a nocturnal stimulus might have on dream content if it were related to a specific stressful presleep event. We showed all our subjects a stressful film just before they went to sleep. The film depicted three workshop accidents. In the first, the tip of a worker's finger was cut off by a jointer (there was a close-up of the bleeding finger). In the second, half of a worker's finger was cut off by an edge saw. And in the third accident a worker was killed by a board shot from a circular saw. He was shown dying on the floor, impaled by the board.

For half of the subjects, we played a portion of the sound track, through a speaker near their heads, just after each REM period began until twenty seconds before we awakened them to collect their dreams. The sound track contained the voice of the main character in the film. He was bemoaning his own negligence which resulted in the third accident in which his fellow worker was killed. While he spoke there was the sound of a circular saw in the background, The other half of the subjects received no sound stimulation.

Oddly enough, there was only one instance of direct incorporaton of the sound stimulus itself. Nonetheless, the stimulus did have an impact on the content of dreams. Those subjects who heard the sound track while they slept dreamed more about aspects of the film than the subjects who had no sound stimulation. Here is an excerpt from a dream occurring during the sound stimulation condition:

S: . . . I was at school, I think, or at a school I don't know where. It might have been the school that I went to because the landscape looked the same. Anyway I was outside the schoolyard, so was another teacher. Oh no, that was not the case. I was in a fort or something and after that I had a regiment of men under me. They were clothed in military uniform of the time of the independence of the states; now we were more or less surrounded by these unfriendly people who themselves were not wearing uniforms, but anyway, I managed to pull some trick that enabled all the soldiers to get out of the fort and into the woods and only left me in the fort. And when I came out of the fort there were about six different men chasing me and they had knives and they were trying to stab me. . . . Through the course of events I managed to get some knives I think by them throwing them at me, occasionally they cut me. . . . As it turned out the pursuers changed into one person who is a friend of mine, his name is R. and we cut each other a couple of times. The cuts were only on the face. They didn't really look like cuts they looked like abrasions. . . . I decided when we were going back to the school that he had better go back to the school first and wash himself or wash the blood off himself and bring me a washcloth so I could wash the blood off myself. However, what happened instead we went into a place where I guess I was rooming, a sort of dark old place, we went into the back door, it was a screen door with a sort of porch in the back where there was a Franklin pot bellied stove and there was also a pail of water and a kettle. . . . I had filled up the kettle, put it on the stove to heat up the water and when the water was warm I dipped the cloth in it and then. . . . I put some water in the basin and put the cloth in the basin and I walked out of this place where I was boarding . . . and when I walked out of there I walked into the University Center into the downstairs section although the University Center was somewhat remodeled, it had some aspects of the architecture building. There was a table in the men's washroom. I took the rag and the washcloth with me into the washroom and proceeded to fill the basin with water and wash my face. In the washroom there were about four guys and one of them I remember, he was a guy I met when I was in political science. His name was P. He and another guy were sort of rolling around on the floor, I think they were involved in some sort of sexual play although they had all their clothes on but I had the impression that it was that . . . anyway they fooled around with that for a while and I was washing all the blood off my face and the wounds when I washed them off still had blood coming, sort of seeping through the skin. I waited around the washroom tapping the blood off my face waiting for it to coagulate. . . . It did finally stop running and somehow I got to that sequence of events where I was going to go to the show with another friend W. and my wife and daughter. I am not sure how I got from one sequence to the other, whether the scene just faded away and I saw myself in the new scene. . . . Then we were going to the show and that was the point you woke me up. . . .[12]

In this dream, elements from the film such as knives, cuts and blood are clearly and openly represented. In fact, it also appears that the context in which the elements were seen (that is in a film, at a university laboratory) is itself represented by the reference to "going to a show" and the numerous allusions to school and the university. In short, dreams of this type would seem to indicate that external stimulation can influence dream content by virtue of the stimulation's associations to previous waking events.

The studies we've described up to now have shown that while we are sleeping our dreams can both reflect and deflect the potency of environmental stimuli that impinge on us. Another interesting question, which I've already alluded to, is can we learn to respond in a specific, prescribed manner to stimuli presented while we sleep? The answer to this question would not only further the understanding of our relationship to the environment while we sleep, but as we shall see might have some practical implications as well.

LEARNING WHILE ASLEEP

As Fred Evans and his colleagues[13] noted, studies concerned with learning during sleep may be conveniently grouped into three categories. They are sleep to sleep studies, wake to sleep studies and sleep to wake studies.

Sleep to Sleep Studies

Sleep to sleep studies involve an exploration of whether or not we are capable of learning *while* asleep to make specific responses or discriminations *during* sleep.

To examine this question, Evans and his group designed a series of studies in which subjects were required to both receive and respond to verbal cues while they continued to sleep. In order to do this, they gave sub-jects suggestions that required a clearly identifiable action while they slept. For example, one suggestion was, "Whenever I say the word 'pillow' your pillow will feel un-comfortable and you will want to move it with your hand." Another one was, "Whenever I say the word 'itch' your nose will itch until you scratch it." In the final study[14] of the series, they also included dummy words to see if subjects would be able to discriminate between the relevant and irrelevant stimuli. While responses were not obtained all of the time, nor from all of the subjects, there were a number of interesting findings. First, the sugges-tion was successful only if it was administered during REM sleep and only if the cue word was administered dur-ing REM sleep. Second, subjects were able to respond to the cue words alone when they returned to the laboratory some five months after the initial training. Third, the sub-jects were able to discriminate between the meaningful cue words and the dummy words. And fourth, the sub-jects had no waking memory for the cue words presented during the night.

Wake to Sleep Studies

Wake to sleep studies are designed to investigate whether or not instructions or training given while awake can be acted upon while asleep. For example, subjects in one study[15] were rewarded if they could awaken themselves "completely" when they heard a telephone ringing or bagpipes playing. At various times during the night these sounds, or other neutral ones such as the sound of a doorbell ringing or airplanes going by, were played through a speaker system. The subjects could per-form this task quite well, providing some additional evidence that we are in fact able to both make discrimina-tions and provide a predetermined response to them while we are asleep.

There is one other wake to sleep study I want to men-tion. It was an attempt through presleep training and REM stimulation to learn about the content of dreams directly from the dreamer as they were taking place. To do this Mario Bertini and his associates in Rome[16] had their subjects come to the laboratory for an hour-long training session on each of ten successive days. During the training sessions, they lay in a darkened room and white noise was played into their ears every ten minutes for several minutes at a time. The subjects were instructed to say whatever came to mind when they heard the white noise. After the training sessions were over, the subjects came to the laboratory to stay the night. When they were in their REM periods, the white noise was again played into their ears. In many cases, the white noise awakened the subjects, but in some cases they produced verbalizations without awakening, verbalizations that may have been accounts of ongoing dreams. Although more work of this nature needs to be done, this study along with those of Evans and his colleagues raises the intriguing possibility of communicating directly with the individual while he or she remains asleep.

Sleep to Wake Studies

Sleep to wake studies were designed to explore the possibility that we could learn something while we sleep that we could subsequently utilize during our waking lives. This certainly was an intriguing proposition. Since we spend about a third of our lives sleeping, it would be very nice if we could use that time to some "practical" advantage. Indeed, there were many commercial outfits that suggested that the "wasted" time asleep could be usefully spent ingesting vast amounts of information which could later be exploited during waking life. A burgeoning industry promised everything from language learning to personality improvement during the time spent asleep.

Sad to say, easy learning during sleep, which subsequently can be put into operation when we are awake, just doesn't seem to be a possibility. In a couple of classic studies[17] Emmons and Simon gave their subjects a series of questions on general knowledge. From these questions, they compiled a list made up only of questions their subjects were unable to answer. During the course of the night, they played the questions along with the correct answers over and over again. The next morning, they tested their subjects. Essentially, no learning took place while the subjects were asleep. The only questions the subjects were able to answer correctly were those they happened to hear in moments of wakefulness or when they were in a drowsy state as they drifted off to sleep.

In a slightly different type of study,[18] an attempt was made to see if material presented during sleep could make learning of the same material quicker or more efficient on morning waking. Accordingly, subjects heard twenty repetitions of a list of pairs of nonsense syllables during the course of the night. The next morning, these subjects could learn the pairings no more quickly than another group of subjects who had been exposed to random musical noise during the course of the previous night. As you might expect, the authors concluded that there was no evidence that learning can take place during sleep, although they suggested information may be absorbed and retained during the drowsy state.

But perhaps this is a slight misstatement of the case. It is probably more accurate to say that we can absorb and retain information while we're sleeping but we simply can't recall it when we wake up. The material still may be there, but we are not able to gain access to it. A good example of this can be found in the studies by Evans and his colleagues that we just discussed. In those studies, subjects were able to perform the designated tasks on hearing the cue words they learned while they were asleep, but on waking, they had no recollection of the cue words. The fact that they could respond to the cue words on the next night, or even on a night five months later, is good evidence that they had absorbed and retained the material while asleep. The big question then, is why wasn't it available to them when they were awake? As we'll see in the next chapter, the answer to that question has a great deal of relevance for understanding dream recall and dream recall failure.

8

Dream Recall and Dream Recall Failure

In a very real sense the question of dream recall and dream recall failure was not of great concern to Freud. As he said:

> The forgetting of dreams, too, remains inexplicable unless the power of psychical censorship is taken into account. In a number of cases the feeling of having dreamt a great deal during the night and of only having retained a little of it may in fact have some other meaning, such as that the dream-work has been perceptibly proceeding all through the night but has left only a short dream behind. . . . It is no doubt true that we forget dreams more and more as time passes after waking; we often forget them in spite of the most painstaking efforts to recall them. But I am of the opinion that the extent of this forgetting is as a rule overestimated; and there is a similar overestimation of the extent to which the gaps in a dream limit our knowledge of it. It is often possible by means of analysis to restore all that has been lost by the forgetting of the dream's content; at least, in quite a number of cases one can reconstruct from a single remaining fragment not, it is true, the dream—which in any case is a matter of no importance—but all the dream thoughts.[1]

As you can see, Freud believed that the amount of dream forgetting was generally exaggerated. He thought instances when the dreamer could remember only a short dream yet felt he or she had been dreaming throughout the night were probably attributable to the dreamer being aware of the *process* of dream creation which in fact left only a short dream behind.

Freud believed these relatively few instances when dreams were forgotten or only a fragment retained could be easily explained. If you recall, according to Freud (chapter 2) it is during sleep that censorship is most lax, that unconscious wishes are most likely to gain entrance into consciousness, albeit in a disguised form, in the content of our dreams. On waking, the full powers of censorship are reconstituted. Consequently, insofar as the dreamwork did not adequately disguise these unacceptable, unconscious wishes, the dream or the offending parts of the dream would likely be expelled from consciousness (repressed) when the dreamer awakened. The dream is likely to be drawn back "into oblivion."[2]

Of course, Freud was not privy to the information we have now, namely that we dream at least four or five times a night. Yet, as we've already noted, under normal circumstances at home we remember on average only one dream every two nights.[3] Dream forgetting is obviously more than just an occasional event!

How then do we account for this high incidence of dream recall failure? Is the repression of dreams simply a much more prevalent phenomenon than Freud imagined? Or are there other explanations for our failure to recall dreams? And why is it that we are so readily able to recall dreams during a night in the laboratory but not during a night at home?

INVESTIGATIONS OF REPRESSION

Investigating the concept of repression, particularly repression of dreams, is a difficult way to earn a living.

The main problem is of course that once a dream is repressed, it is generally lost to the dreamer forever. But ironically, the most compelling evidence for the existence of repression would first involve recovery of the repressed dream and then a demonstration that the material in the dream had indeed constituted some sort of psychological threat to the dreamer.

Consequently, most of the evidence for repression has been of a presumptive nature. For example, Wolpert[4] cited a number of clinical examples of dream material recovered during the course of psychoanalytic treatment which might provide some slight evidence for the existence of repression. In addition, there are a couple of studies like that of Whitman and his colleagues[5] which investigated the nature of dream recall in relation to the listener. Their subjects participated in laboratory experiments at the same time they were undergoing psychotherapy. Whitman and his colleagues found there were occasions the subjects reported some dreams to the experimenter and others to the therapist and vice versa. They speculated that these dreams might have caused some discomfort if related to a particular listener (generally the psychiatrist) and as a result may have been repressed.

Implicit in this last study is the basic assumption that has guided some of our own attempts to explore and define the limits of the role of repression in dream forgetting, namely that it is the most emotionally charged or affectful dreams that are the best candidates for repression. This assumption fits nicely with the fact that there is much more dream recall in the laboratory than at home. As it turns out, in general, laboratory dreams are accompanied by less emotion than home dreams.[6] This being the case, it's logical to assume that repression is more likely to occur for home dreams than laboratory dreams. This in turn could account for at least some of the differences found in the amount of dream recall obtained in the two situations.

A second, and related, assumption is that emotionally charged presleep experiences would increase the emotion in the dreams of the night and result in increased dream recall failure due to repression. Both Goodenough[7] and I[8] suggested that a specific type of waking report might be indicative of repression having taken place. The report, which we designated as an "ND" or no-content dream report, is characterized by subjects saying they know they *had* been dreaming but can no longer remember the content of their dreams. This type of report is distinct from an "N" report, one in which the subjects say they had *not* been dreaming at all prior to being awakened.

Our assumptions were somewhat bolstered by our own findings that there was an increase in no-content dream reports after the viewing of stressful presleep films. Another study[9] indicated that contentless and vague dream reports were more likely to occur after stress, especially for people who generally recalled dreams infrequently. Finally, the results of still another study[10] were also encouraging. In that study it was found that in about one third of the recall failures of subjects prone to use repression as their major mechanism of defense, the subjects spontaneously reported having had no-content dreams. Although they obviously couldn't recall the content of these dreams, the subjects generally reported the unremembered dreams seemed to have been bizarre and marked by a high degree of emotion.

While these findings were limited in scope, they were intriguing and provided the impetus for more systematic investigations of the repression notion. In particular we reasoned that if no-content dream reports were accompanied by some sort of measurable indices of high emotionality, we would have substantial evidence to support our assumption that highly charged dreams are good candidates for repression and that the ND report is itself indicative of repression having taken place.

Fortunately for us, such indices did exist. As I mentioned earlier (chapter 4), dreams accompanied by increased respiration rates were often characterized by increased amounts of hostility, depression and anxiety. In addition, dreams containing greater amounts of hostility and anxiety were often accompanied by a greater number of eye movements than dreams devoid of these emotions. In other words, both eye movement and respiration rates increased when there were increases in the emotionality of reported dreams.

This evidence that eye movement activity and breathing during REM sleep are related to emotionality in reported dreams made it reasonable to assume that the same measures would also signify emotionality in dreams when there is dream recall failure. Accordingly, we used the subincision and birth films (chapter 4) as presleep experiences in an attempt to increase the emotionality of the dreams of the night. Then we compared respiration measures and eye movement activity for those REM periods that yielded dream reports and those that did not.[11]

In general, REM periods that led to *dreamless* sleep reports were characterized by fewer eye movements and slower breathing. However, much to our surprise, REM periods that led to *no-content* dream reports showed more regular breathing than REM periods from which dreams were obtained. In short, our physiological indices indicated the dreams that were least likely to be recalled on awakening, including our vaunted NDs, were those accompanied by little or no emotion.

What's more, we found similar results when we examined our subjects' ability to re-recall their dreams of the night the following morning. It was precisely those dreams that had been characterized as having little affect by the subjects during the night that were subsequently most likely to be forgotten in the morning. On the other hand, those dreams that were accompanied by the greatest amount of negative emotion during the night were the ones most likely to be remembered the following morning.

These findings that emotionally charged dreams in the laboratory are the ones that are best recalled run counter to a repression explanation of dream recall failure. However, they are consistent with a salience explanation of *successful* dream recall.

SALIENCE

According to the salience notion,[12] dreams that are relatively high in novelty, bizarreness, vividness, emotionality and the like will be more likely to stand out in an array of experiences. Consequently, they will be more readily remembered than dreams that are more mundane and less vivid or affectful.

The salience notion suggests the importance of the dream to the dreamer and its emotional charge might serve to insulate the dream against distractions that may occur on awakening. And indeed, there are many possible sources of distraction. For example, in the laboratory, our stressful films provide a possible source of distraction. On being awakened during the course of the night, the subjects' attention may tend to be drawn to those stressful presleep events. Even the attention and effort necessary to find the phone in response to our awakening buzzer might serve as a source of distraction. In fact, we now know that simply assigning people tasks to perform on waking, thus creating a distraction, makes it more difficult for them to recall their dreams.[13]

While the focus of the salience notion has been on the nature of the dreams that are best suited to override the intrusion of distracting events, it obviously has implications for the types of dreams most likely to be relegated to the nether regions of our memories. As I mentioned before, we would expect such dreams to be relatively mundane, less vivid and less emotional. But where and how can we find evidence for a proposition such as this?

In a now classic study of dream recall,[14] Don Goodenough and his colleagues set out to investigate possible differences between so-called dream recallers and nonrecallers. The nonrecallers were people who reported they rarely recalled dreams at home, that is, they recalled fewer than one a month. The recallers, on the other hand, reported they recalled dreams almost every night.

The first thing Goodenough and his colleagues ascertained was that both of these groups of people spent the same amount of time in REM periods. So there were no differences between the groups in their sleep patterns that might have accounted for the differences in dream recall. While every subject remembered at least one dream during the three nights they spent in the laboratory, the recallers remembered far more dreams than the nonrecallers.

In casting about for reasons for this difference in recall, Goodenough and his colleagues came up with an interesting possibility. They wondered if the nonrecallers might be prone to mislabel the experience of dreaming. This idea came to them as a result of some experiences they had with their nonrecallers. For example, one of their subjects, on arriving at the laboratory, reported he had never dreamed. Consequently, he wondered how he would know if he had been dreaming when he was awakened. While this may seem like a rather strange question, as the authors pointed out, it really was perfectly reasonable coming from a person who has never recalled a dream before. Other nonrecallers were sometimes not sure if they had been asleep and dreaming or awake and thinking, and yet another nonrecaller reported he had been asleep and thinking when awakened from a REM period.*

Speculating on these interchanges with their subjects, Goodenough and his colleagues wondered whether the designation of dreams as thoughts might in fact reflect the quality of much of the dream content of nonrecallers. Perhaps their dreams were in fact generally more thoughtlike and mundane, and hence more likely to be blotted out by the distractions of waking life.

To examine this possibility, Bernice Barber[15] collected a number of dreams from people who claimed they dreamed often and others who indicated they seldom if ever dreamed. To collect the dreams she awakened her subjects towards the end of their nights' sleep by calling them at home on a telephone placed beside their beds. Naturally, it took a long time to collect a sufficient number of dreams from the nonrecallers while it was relatively easy to collect dreams from the recallers.

Independent judges rated all the dreams for a number of different characteristics. As expected, they found the dreams of the nonrecallers were typically more mundane and thoughtlike than those of the recallers. Then Barber went a step further. She gave transcripts of the dreams to a number of different people and asked them to recount the dreams from memory. She found the dreams of the nonrecallers were less readily remembered than those of the recallers.

---

*As a result of experiences such as these, we changed our instructions to the subjects in all our subsequent studies. Now on waking the subjects we ask, "Was anything going through your mind, just prior to the buzzer sounding?" instead of, "Were you dreaming just prior to the buzzer sounding?" This small change eliminated the problem of subjects being required to make a decision as to whether or not they were dreaming. They're simply asked to let us know if anything had been occurring just prior to being awakened and to recount as much of it as they are able to remember.

In short, Barber confirmed that at least a portion of dream recall and dream recall failure can be accounted for by the nature of the dream content itself. Some dreams are simply intrinsically more memorable than others, probably in part because they are insulated from distractions on waking, including the potential distractions of memories of other dreams of the night.

However, the nature of a particular dream's content is not the only determinant of whether or not it will be remembered the next morning. The position of a dream in an array of dreams of the night, as well as how many dreams have actually occurred during the night, also play roles in the likelihood that a given dream will be remembered. Not surprisingly, these aspects of dream recall and dream recall failure follow from a basic precept found in the literature on waking memory, namely, the concept of interference.

INTERFERENCE

A good deal of the work on waking memory has been concerned with factors that may account for the success and/or failure of recall of previously learned material. Some of this work has focused on what has come to be known as the serial-position effect. Let's say you were given a list of similar items to read once. A list of about ten, random, two-digit numbers or so would be a good example. Then you were asked to recall them. You would most likely be able to remember the first and last numbers without any trouble but you'd probably have some difficulty with the numbers in the middle. That would be an example of the serial-position effect. The position of the number in the list played a role in determining whether or not it was remembered.

Of course, if the list of numbers had been very short, you would have had little difficulty in remembering most, if not all, of the numbers. The serial-position effect would have been muted. So how does all this apply to dream recall?

Our ability to recall material coming at the beginning of a list of similar items better than material coming in the middle is referred to as the primacy effect. In the case of dreams, the first dreams of the night are more readily re-recalled the next morning than dreams occurring in the middle of the night.[16]

The recency effect refers to the fact that we are also better able to recall material coming at the end of a list of similar items than material coming in the middle of the list. Again, as far as dreams are concerned, the last dreams of the night are more likely to be re-recalled in the morning than dreams coming in the middle of the night.[17]

Finally as we've mentioned, the length of the list also plays a role in the likelihood of a single item being recalled—the shorter the list, the greater the likelihood that a given item will be recalled. Such an effect has also been demonstrated in the case of dream recall. For example, Meier and his colleagues[18] studied one subject over a forty-five–night period. They reported the subject had less difficulty re-recalling his dreams in the morning when there were only a few of them, but morning recall became more difficult when many dreams had been reported the previous night.

Interestingly enough, within the context of interference we can also better understand why emotional dreams are more readily remembered in the morning than their less emotional counterparts. For example, if in the original list of random, two-digit numbers you were given, one three-digit number was included, you probably would have little difficulty in remembering it, no matter where it was placed in the list. This is because the number would stand out. Its dissimilarity from the rest of the numbers would make it more memorable. Similarly, as I've already mentioned, dreams that stand out because of their high emotionality relative to the other dreams of the night are more likely to be re-recalled on the following morning.

In short, it's clear that the nature of the dream, its position among an array of dreams and the total number of dreams of a night all play a role in determining the likelihood that a given dream will be recalled the next morning. However, we still have a problem. How can we account for the huge discrepancy between the number of dreams obtained in the laboratory and the number normally remembered at home? Indeed, as we've already noted, home dream reports are generally more emotionally charged than laboratory reports. Within the context of the salience notion, we would expect that home dream recall should be superior to laboratory recall. Of course the reverse is true. One possible explanation lies with the peculiar procedure generally used to collect dreams in the laboratory—abrupt awakenings during REM periods.

AROUSAL

Arousal is a general term we've used to describe the soup to nuts of awakening. For example, arousal includes ever-so-slight, momentary changes in the EEG pattern indicating a transient instant of awakening. But it also includes the abrupt, sometimes jolting awakenings produced by our alarm clocks at home or the experimenter's bell in the laboratory. It includes moments of awakening that we aren't aware have taken place. But it also includes prolonged periods of wakefulness during the course of the night. In short, the term arousal refers to a whole range of awakenings from slight to profound and of long and short duration.

Evidence for the role of arousal in dream recall actually comes from two different sources. The first is studies of the arousal procedure itself. The second is studies concerned with learning during sleep.

To examine the abrupt awakening procedure, Shapiro and his colleagues[19] awakened subjects from their REM periods with either an extremely loud bell or else a soft tone which was gradually increased in intensity until the subjects ultimately awakened. They found that the abrupt awakenings were more likely to elicit reports of dreams, while the gradual awakenings were more likely to elicit thoughtlike reports. They also found that dream recall was more likely to be obtained from awakenings that took place later in the night.

This latter finding is of particular interest because it fits nicely with the information we have on awakening thresholds.[20] In general the more sleep we have, the more easily we are awakened. Consequently, we would expect that abrupt awakenings would be more readily obtained later in the night, precisely when dream recall is best.*

The importance of arousal in dream recall is highlighted by some of the studies on sleep learning we discussed in the last chapter. As you'll recall, those studies indicated that memory for material presented during sleep only took place if the subjects were awakened, albeit briefly, by the stimuli. Other studies also have implicated arousal as an important element for the subsequent memory of material presented during sleep. For example, memory of words and tones presented during sleep is related to the duration of the arousal produced by the stimuli.[21]

Taking a slightly different tack, Goodenough and his colleagues[22] awakened subjects a number of times during the course of a night. At the time of the awakening, the subjects were asked to read a word in the belief that the speed of their response was a measure of their alertness. Then they were either kept awake by performing such

---

*In light of the information we now have, it seems there are also other reasons the dreams we recall at home are most likely to come from the last REM period of the night. Since REM periods increase in length as the night progresses, there is every likelihood that our alarm clocks, causing an abrupt awakening, will sound during the last REM period. Also, the dream occurring at that time will have an added advantage in being recalled because it is the last dream of the night.

tasks as playing a pinball game, or they were allowed to return to sleep right away. It was found that words followed by periods of arousal were better remembered the next morning than words followed immediately by sleep. These results suggested that sleep itself inhibits subsequent waking memory, a finding that has obvious implications for the morning recall of dreams. What's more, these results dovetail nicely with the findings that arousal during dreaming aids in subsequent morning dream recall.

RETRIEVING DREAMS

From our discussion up to now, it's apparent that many diverse factors combine to aid or hinder our ability to recall dreams. In order to describe the complicated interplay between these factors, Don Goodenough and I advanced an arousal-retrieval model of dream recall and dream recall failure.[23] Our basic premise was that there are two major steps involved in the dream recall process. The first step entails the dream being formed in our memories in a state amenable to being recalled. The second step concerns our ultimate ability to retrieve the dream on waking.

Turning once again to the classical literature on learning and memory, we speculated that initially dreams reside in a short-term memory system or storage. The dream material is then transferred to a long-term storage. The manner in which the dream is transferred plays a profound role in whether it is amenable to recall the following morning.

Here the work on arousal and sleep learning comes into play. We believe that arousal, even brief arousal, occurring while the dream is taking place, enables us to place it in long-term storage in a form compatible with retrieval during the waking state. Conversely, the transfer of the dream in a form amenable to retrieval is inhibited by sleep. However, the fact that a dream is placed in long-term storage in a form amenable to waking recall does not in and of itself insure that it will be recalled on waking. At that time, the dream is subject to the vagaries of distraction and interference I described earlier. If it is mundane, or if it has occurred in the middle of an array of dreams or if there are compelling thoughts or events on waking, the dream is still likely to be lost.

This conceptualization can account for the relatively high dream recall and re-recall rate we obtain in the laboratory. Goodenough and I speculated that abrupt awakenings "catch" the dream while it is still in short-term storage, before any processing has taken place. The arousal for the purpose of dream collection in turn aids in the transfer of the dream into long-term storage in a form amenable to waking recall.

The fact that any dreams at all are recalled at home presents no problem for this model. There of course can be fortuitous awakenings by an alarm clock or the like during REM periods, which would function in a manner similar to the experimenter's awakening buzzer in the laboratory. But we also know that there are spontaneous awakenings during the night. These awakenings can provide sufficient arousal time to permit the successful transfer of material into long-term storage. Interestingly enough, as we have seen, dreams containing a relatively high degree of emotion are often associated with brief periods of arousal (chapter 5), which is another reason that such dreams are the ones most likely to be recalled the next morning. Finally, within this context it's interesting to note that one of the differences between dream recallers and nonrecallers is that the former group of people reports having far more spontaneous awakenings during the night than does the latter group.[24]

So where does that leave the notion of repression? In our model, we suggested that if repression does take place, it becomes a factor only in attempts at retrieval of a dream from long-term storage. As we have seen, attempts to explore repression in the laboratory have met with failure. Perhaps this is because dreams occurring in the laboratory are generally not *extremely* emotional and the awakening procedure taps the short-term storage subverting the possible effects of repression.

However, there is one home dream study that may have some bearing on the question.[25] In that study, I examined the home dream recall of forty-five subjects. Since an earlier study[26] had revealed that dream emotionality is related to morning mood, I asked my subjects to fill out a questionnaire indicating how they felt in the morning. I then asked them to indicate how many dreams they had had during the night. Finally I asked them to describe in as much detail as possible all of the dreams they were able to remember. I found the greatest number of no-content dream reports came when the subjects reported having either very little or very much affect in the morning. The smallest number of no-content dreams came from those subjects who reported having a moderate amount of emotionality on waking in the morning. Assuming that morning mood was indeed related to the emotionality of dreams, the results of this study are consistent with the hypothesis that dreams accompanied by little emotion are lost because of lack of salience, while those accompanied by a great deal of emotion may be lost because of repression.

Even if this is the case, it seems clear that the role of repression in dream recall failure is not nearly as important in explaining dream recall failure as Freud thought. If repression does indeed take place it is only one of many factors making dream recall under normal circumstances an extremely elusive process.

9

Dream Deprivation

So up to now we've seen that dreams can reflect the events and the emotions of the day. They can be reactions to words and sounds impinging on us while we sleep. They are even at times responsive to changes in our bodies, changes of which we may not ourselves be aware. And we have also seen that dreams are a regularly occurring part of our sleeping lives. But does this mean that dreams have a purpose or usefulness in the context of our waking lives? Or to put it another way, do we need to dream?

This is not an easy question to answer. Freud himself would have probably considered this question as singularly unimportant. For example, he quoted with apparent derision Purkinje's view of the reviving and healing function of dreams:

> These functions are performed especially by productive dreams. They are the easy play of the imagination and have no connection with the affairs of daytime. The mind has no wish to prolong the tensions of waking life; it seeks to relax them and to recover from them. It produces above all conditions contrary to the waking ones. It cures sorrow by joy, cares by hopes and pictures of happy distraction,

hatred by love and friendliness, fear by courage and foresight; it allays doubt by conviction and firm faith, and vain expectation by fulfilment. Many of the spirit's wounds which are being constantly re-opened during the day are healed by sleep, which covers them and shields them from fresh injury. The healing action of time is based partly on this.[1]

Freud then went on to comment, "We all have a feeling that sleep has a beneficial effect upon mental activities, and the obscure working of the popular mind refuses to let itself be robbed of its belief that dreaming is one of the ways in which sleep dispenses its benefits."[2]

These views of Freud are not really very surprising. After all, as we discovered earlier (chapter 2), for Freud the main function of dreams in waking life was as an interpretive tool. They were the means for unlocking the mysteries of the unconscious. As he put it, *"The interpretation of dreams is the royal road to the knowledge of the unconscious activities of the mind."*[3] During sleep, of course, Freud believed dreams served primarily as protection from the intrusion of unacceptable infantile wishes which might awaken us.

With the discovery of the sleep cycle and its regularly occurring REM periods, there seemed to be an ideal means for exploring questions about the function of dreams. Based on the assumption that most of our dreaming occurs during REM periods, one possible way of going about answering such questions would be to take away or at least limit the occurrence of REM periods and see what happens.

Indeed some of the work we discussed earlier involving drugs and alcohol (chapter 6) held promise that this type of investigation might be quite fruitful. If you recall, most sleeping pills as well as alcohol reduce the ·time spent in REM periods. When these substances were withdrawn, there was a resultant increase in the percent of sleep time spent in REM periods. That is, there was a

REM rebound. These findings certainly would seem to indicate that we need to spend a certain amount of time in REM sleep. When it is taken away, we strive to recover it.

Some of the work with alcoholics was particularly dramatic.[4] Not only did they have inordinate amounts of REM sleep during the night when alcohol was withdrawn but they also had frightening hallucinations while awake.* It was almost as if the immense suppression of REM sleep resulted in a spill over of dreaming activity into the waking state.

REM DEPRIVATION

Depriving people of REM sleep is not as simple as it may sound. It requires a great deal of vigilance and perseverance on the part of the experimenter and particularly large quantity of patience on the part of the subject.

In general, the procedures used in REM deprivation studies are the same as those used in dream studies. Subjects are hooked up to an EEG machine and they are allowed to go to sleep. They are awakened by a loud buzzer or bell or by having their name called just as if dream collection was going to take place. However, in the deprivation studies, instead of waiting for the REM period to progress for some time, the experimenter attempts to awaken the subject at the very beginning of each and every REM period.

Obviously experimenters involved in this type of work had to be ever alert to the changing EEG patterns which might herald a REM period (chapter 3). But they had to be even more alert than one might have expected. As it turned out, during the course of REM deprivation experimenters had to awaken their subjects with ever-

---

*These visual hallucinations are called delirium tremens or "DT's."

increasing frequency—ten or more times on the first night was not unusual![5] As the nights of deprivation continued, even more awakenings were likely to be necessary.

What's more, it often became essential to keep the subjects up for some time after the awakening to prevent them from immediately falling back into REM sleep. Usually, as you might guess, it also became increasingly difficult for the experimenters to awaken their subjects.

A drastic example of these difficulties was reported by Dement and Fisher.[6] They had to end an experiment with one subject after twelve nights of REM deprivation because it became virtually impossible to awaken him. The only way they could successfully arouse him and prevent him from immediately going back into REM sleep was to haul him from his bed and walk him around until he was fully awake.

Obviously, this was a rather extreme and unusual situation. Nevertheless, it's no wonder that under conditions such as these the forbearance of dedicated and understanding subjects was an essential ingredient to completing any prolonged REM deprivation experiment. With all the turmoil surrounding the subjects, it's really surprising how minor the effects of REM deprivation ultimately proved to be. For example, some subjects report having increased appetites. In fact, in one study,[7] a subject reported having a sudden desire for roast duck. He promptly bought one, roasted it and ate it. In another study[8] subjects were REM deprived by awakenings for a five-night period. They became somewhat anxious and irritable. In still another study,[9] subjects were deprived of REM sleep by strong electrical shocks to the foot for a seven-day period. These subjects exhibited an increased amount of irritability.* Wouldn't you?

---

*Another group of subjects were deprived of stage 4 sleep for seven nights by the same procedure. They exhibited an increase in depression.

In short, these minimal findings of increases in appetite or slight increases in anxiety and irritability made it difficult to draw any firm conclusions about the possible functions of REM sleep. Obviously, the invasiveness of the REM deprivation procedures themselves might have been responsible for the changes in mood that were observed. In addition, by definition prolonged REM deprivation also inevitably involved at least some sleep deprivation. The subjects had to be awakened more frequently as the experiments progressed and in some instances had to be kept awake. Could the slight changes observed in daytime functioning not have resulted from the general sleep loss rather than from the lack of REM sleep itself?

In spite of problems associated with this type of research, two important findings emerged from the REM deprivation studies. First, as the duration of REM deprivation increased, attempts to have REM sleep increased. Second, when subjects were allowed to sleep through the night* after REM deprivation, there were profound increases in the percent of time spent in REM sleep. Taken together, these facts indicated some sort of pressure or need to have REM sleep.

There are some other studies that demonstrated this pressure for REM sleep in an even more dramatic fashion. In one study,[10] cats were allowed to sleep for prescribed amounts of time for a period of up to twenty days. The total sleep time the cats were allowed varied from as much as twelve hours to only two hours a day. But regardless of the total amount of sleep time, REM time remained almost constant. As the total sleep time decreased, the percentage of REM time increased.

In another study,[11] the amount of REM time was recorded for two subjects over a number of nights before the experimental procedure began. Then they were REM

---

*These nights of undisturbed sleep after the cessation of an experimental procedure are referred to as "recovery nights."

deprived. After this, they had five more nights of sleep in which the amount of REM sleep was maintained at its original, pre-experimental level. Finally, they were permitted to have recovery sleep. In spite of the intervening five nights, on the recovery night there was an increase in the percentage of REM sleep. The amount of REM recovery was similar to the amount that would have been expected if the recovery night had occurred immediately after the deprivation.

In still another study,[12] an entirely different tack was taken. This study capitalized on the findings we discussed earlier that subjects are able to respond to stimuli while they sleep. The subjects had a switch taped to their hands. They were told that when they heard a tone during the night, they were to press the switch three times. They were also told that they might be awakened at various times during the night. Unbeknownst to the subjects the tone was always presented during the last two and a half hours of sleep. For some subjects the tones were presented during stage 2 sleep. For other subjects they were presented during REM sleep. Some of the subjects were REM deprived until the last two and a half hours of sleep while the others were not. Some of the subjects were awakened by calling their names if they failed to respond to the tone, while other subjects were not.

As it turned out, subjects were more likely to press the switch during stage 2 sleep as opposed to REM sleep when they heard the tone if they were *not* awakened. However, awakening for failure to provide a response during REM sleep dramatically increased the likelihood the subjects would respond during REM sleep, while it made no difference in the number of responses during stage 2 sleep. What is more, when the subjects were deprived of REM sleep, but not awakened after failing to respond, they only responded about one percent of the time. However, after the REM deprivation procedure when they were awakened for failing to press the switch, on subsequent trials they responded eighty-five percent of the time. In short, when the sanctity of REM sleep was threatened, the subjects were more likely to press the switch to avoid an awakening. This likelihood increased as the need for REM sleep increased as a result of REM deprivation.

So all of these studies illustrated the apparent need to have a full complement of REM sleep. In the first study, REM sleep was more or less maintained at its normal level over a period of nights even though the total sleep time was altered. In the second study, missing REM sleep was recovered at the first available opportunity, in that case, five days after the end of REM deprivation. Finally, in the third study, response to an intrusive stimulus during REM sleep was limited, except when the stimulus was coupled with the information that it had the potential to interfere with the subject's ability to remain in REM sleep.

Studies of total sleep deprivation also provide some indication of the importance of REM sleep. When our sleep is curtailed either by events beyond our control or by choice,* sleep on subsequent nights is altered in characteristic ways. Generally, total sleep deprivation is followed by prolonged periods of stage 4 sleep at the beginning of the recovery night. There is usually a con-commitant delay in the appearance of REM sleep.[13] In fact, the missing REM sleep might even be made up a night or two later. This is especially true if the sleep deprivation period is a particularly lengthy one. But whether or not there is a delay in the recovery of REM sleep, ultimately at least some of it will be recouped.

This type of postdeprivation reorganization of sleep was clearly illustrated in a study[14] involving four volunteers. These subjects were totally deprived of sleep

---

*My students often insist that the all-night "cram" sessions they spend studying for my exams are my doing. I'm just as insistent that it's their choice. Either way, when they do get to bed, we can be sure the organization of their sleep patterns will be dramatically different from their organization under normal circumstances.

for 205 hours. After the deprivation their sleep was recorded in the laboratory for three consecutive nights and compared to their normal sleep patterns obtained prior to
deprivation. It was found that the greatest increase in the
amount of stage 4 sleep occurred on the first recovery
night after the sleep deprivation. While there was also an
increase in the amount of REM sleep on that night, the
greatest increase in REM sleep came a night later, on the
second recovery night. Finally, the extra time spent in
stage 4 sleep and REM sleep on the recovery nights was at
the expense of stage 2 sleep.

Taken together, the findings from these and similar
REM and sleep deprivation studies are quite instructive.
First, they indicate that we undoubtedly need to have a
certain amount of stage 4 and REM sleep. Second, they
suggest that the sleep stages can be ordered in terms of
their relative importance to us. Since after total sleep
deprivation stage 4 sleep is recouped prior to compensation for REM sleep loss, it seems reasonable to assume
that stage 4 sleep is somehow more vital to our functioning than REM sleep. Similarly, the fact that both stage 4
and REM sleep are made up at the expense of stage 2 sleep
would suggest that this latter stage of sleep is of relatively
little importance to us.

In spite of these findings, we are still left with a gnaw-
ing problem concerning REM sleep. Why is it important to
us? Is it the psychological components of the vivid dreams
that accompany REM periods that are crucial to our well-
being? Or is it the particular physiological characteristics
of REM sleep (chapter 3) that are of preeminent importance?

There are a number of theories that have suggested
that it is the physiological components of REM sleep that
are of primary importance to us. For example, one
theory,[15] the "ontogenetic" hypothesis, postulated that
REM sleep provides the necessary stimulation for satisfactory development and maintenance of the central nervous
system. This notion was based on the observation that

REM sleep is a much bigger component of total sleep time in newborn infants than it is later on in life. Two factors were viewed as playing a role in the ultimate reduction in total REM time. First, after the maturation of the cortex there is presumably less need for the stimulation provided by REM sleep. And second, as children spend more time awake they obtain more of the stimulation necessary for maintenance of the cortex from external sources, thus reducing the need for the stimulation provided by REM sleep.

Another theory,[16] the "homeostatic" hypothesis, suggested REMs help to maintain optimal levels of cortical functioning by providing appropriate moments of activation against a background of less activation during non-REM sleep. A third theory,[17] the "sentinel" hypothesis, proposed that REM sleep serves a vigilance function by providing periodic times during sleep when an animal is best able to assess its environment for danger and is most physically prepared to take appropriate action.

As you can imagine, none of these theories has anything of note to say about the dreaming component of REM sleep. The truth of the matter is that scientists who approach the study of sleep from a physiological or biological perspective generally don't attribute much importance to dreaming itself. They often consider it to be an accidental by-product of the physiological activation taking place during REM sleep.[18] A good example of this perspective can be found in the work of Jim Horne[19] at Loughborough University in England. He suggested that ". . . REM sleep is so intertwined within the organization of sleep, counterbalancing the effects of the deeper forms of non-REM sleep, that it cannot be separated out. Dreaming may have evolved to assist this purpose—to help keep the cerebrum entertained . . ." and he concluded, ". . . it is unlikely that we have REM sleep just to dream."[20]

While it is true we might not have REM sleep "just" to dream, dreaming is a rather prominent component of REM sleep. So we are really confronted with a couple of problems. First, is it at all possible to demonstrate that we have a need to dream? And second, if we do have a need to dream, what functions may dreams play in our lives?

Trying to answer the first question is fraught with difficulties. As we've already seen, taking away REM periods and seeing what happens is no solution. First of all, we don't know whether the need to recover REM periods is a function of a need to have the physiological state of REM sleep or a need to dream. In addition, we have no way of knowing whether dreams aborted by the deprivation procedure are not in some way made up during the other stages of sleep that remain. Don't forget, while dreaming is predominantly associated with REM periods, it can and does occur during non-REM sleep.

Obviously, a new strategy to try and assess the need to dream was called for. The best that we could come up with was to use the REM deprivation procedure I've just described and somehow supply a "substitute" for dreaming. If the expected REM rebound were reduced, we would have at least some evidence to suggest that dreaming per se is important, or that we need to have our dreams.

DREAM SUBSTITUTION

Finding an appropriate substitute for dreaming proved to be no simple task. It was hard to know where to begin. It was frankly a guessing game, an attempt to make a priori decisions about which components of dreaming might be most important for us. Could it be the freewheeling thought processes unbridled by the constraints of waking life that are of paramount importance? Or perhaps it is the vivid images which are so characteristic of dreaming? Or maybe it's something else entirely?

One of the more amusing and inventive studies I know of was described by Bill Dement.[21] He and Charles Fisher decided to explore the possibility that dreams might serve to satisfy oral needs. They planned to REM deprive subjects by waking them in the usual manner, just as their REM periods were beginning. Then they planned to give their subjects something to eat.

The first subject they tested told them his favorite food was banana cream pie. Accordingly, Mrs. Fisher baked a banana cream pie and at each awakening the subject was given a piece to eat. As the night progressed, the banana cream pie became less and less appealing to the subject. This was particularly reflected in the last two dream fragments collected from aborted REM periods. In one, the subject dreamed he was given a plate of spaghetti which he was scraping into a garbage can. In the other, the subject dreamed he was feeding the pie to the experimenter! In short, food, or at least banana cream pie, is apparently not a substitute for dreaming.

In another study,[22] an attempt was made to reduce the REM rebound, resulting from REM deprivation, by supplying subjects with a dream substitute during the day. Since hypnotically induced hallucinations are dreamlike but occur in conjunction with a waking EEG pattern[23] they seemed like an ideal substitute for dreams. Accordingly, three subjects had two and half hours of hypnosis following a night of REM deprivation. However, the hypnotically induced hallucinations failed to reduce REM rebound on subsequent nights.

Apparently, hypnotic hallucinations were not an adequate substitute for dreams. But there was also another possibility. Maybe the dream substitute can only function as such if it replaces the dream *at the time of dreaming.* A couple of studies by Roz Cartwright and her colleagues seemed to indicate this may very well be the case.

In the first study,[24] they noticed that different subjects responded differently to the REM deprivation procedure. Some subjects reported more dreamlike content on being awakened immediately after the start of REM periods than others. These subjects also showed less REM rebound on recovery nights than those who produced little dreamlike content when their REM periods were aborted. In general, the more often dreamlike content was

spontaneously produced during the REM deprivation procedure, the less REM rebound there was on the recovery
nights. In other words, it seemed as if some subjects were
able to squeeze enough dreaming into the very beginning
of their REM periods so as to reduce the need for subsequent dreaming later on.

In a follow-up study,[25] subjects were deprived of REM
sleep the first half of the night on two different nights. On
one of the nights, the only thing the subjects were required to do was to report whatever mental activity had
been occurring just prior to the awakenings. The awakenings of course took place at the beginning of each REM
period during the first half of the night. On the other night,
using the same awakening procedure, the subjects were
required to repeat lists of digits backwards and forwards.
It was found that when dream content was obtained there
was less REM rebound on the second half of the night than
when subjects were required to do the digit span task. In
addition, the more dream content reported, the less the
REM rebound, and the better the performance on the digit
span task, the more the REM rebound! In short, when the
subjects were allowed to engage in a dreamlike activity, in
this case reflection on their own dreams, it apparently
acted as a replacement or substitute for dreaming, reducing the need for compensation later in the night.

In a variant of this study, I tried to extend these findings to more than one night.[26] First I recorded the normal
sleep patterns of my six subjects. On the first REM
deprivation night, half of the subjects were given simple
addition problems to work on for ten minutes after each
awakening. The other half were provided with a diffuse
white light while white noise was played into their ears.*
They were asked to say anything that came to mind and
to describe any visual imagery they had during the ten-
minute period. The following night was a recovery night,

---

*As we discussed earlier, this situation provides an environ-
ment conducive to the production of visual imagery.

allowing me to compare the amount of REM sleep to the records from the normal or baseline nights of sleep. On the next night, the conditions were reversed so that my addition people now had the visual imagery session and my imagery people had the addition task. Finally, there was another recovery night. As it turned out, five of the six subjects had less REM rebound after the imagery session than after the addition session. In short, the opportunity to produce some dreamlike content within the context of a night's sleep seemed to reduce the need to make up the REM sleep on a subsequent night.

There's just one other study I want to mention before going on. In that study,[27] subjects were sleep deprived. At intervals during the sleep deprivation they were given various mental tasks to perform. Generally, they could do them quite well even after prolonged periods of sleep deprivation. Finally, they were allowed to go to sleep. After only two hours of sleep, they were awakened and asked to work on the mental tasks again. Not only was their performance terrible, but on several occasions an interesting thing happened. They began to have waking reveries. Why? That is, why, after a couple of hours of sleep and not prior to going to sleep, did they have such reveries? Of course, we can only speculate. But one possibility is that once the action of sleep is set in motion, we need all of its components, including dreaming. From what we know about recovery sleep after total sleep deprivation, we can be relatively certain that the subjects in this study had had no REM sleep in the two hours of sleep they were permitted. Could these reveries be spill overs of missing dreams that need to be made up once the process of sleeping has begun? And if dreams are important within the context of sleep, what is their function? I'll try to answer that question in the next chapter.

10

The Adaptive Function of Dreams

The major difficulty in doing dream research is the fact that we have to go about it in a rather indirect fashion (chapter 1). Our data are merely the memories of events described to us by our dreamer subjects. And as we have seen, in the telling of the dream, in the translation of often visual, sometimes disjointed experiences into a form comprehensible to the researcher there is a large margin for error.

Consequently, our information about dreams is less complete than we would like it to be. The pieces of the puzzle don't all fit together in a neat, interlocking fashion. Perhaps this will always be the case. Nonetheless, at least some of the puzzle is beginning to take shape. It's time to take stock of what we have and speculate a bit about what the completed picture may look like. There's even the possibility that some of our speculations might point us in the direction where additional pieces of the puzzle ultimately can be found.

Freud's[1] notions of dreaming were the starting points for our odyssey through the strange and mysterious world of dreams. It should be apparent by now that at least some of those notions are no longer tenable. As we have seen (chapter 2), Freud's basic tenet was that dreams are caused by unacceptable, infantile wishes surging towards consciousness while we sleep. The dreams represent an attempt to discharge* those wishes in a relatively benign fashion. Thus in Freud's view, the main function of the dream is to provide a forum where undesirable wishes can be acted upon without their *true* and dangerous significance being understood by the dreamer. According to him, the stage is set for the dream to occur when any waking experience chances to meld with these unconscious, unwelcome yearnings which are constantly striving to gain conscious recognition.

Secondarily, he suggested dreams might be caused by somatic stimuli. In this case too, he saw the dream as serving the purpose of disguising the true character and hence the significance of such stimuli to the dreamer. In addition, although of lesser importance, he posited that incursions from the environment could also cause dreams. And here again he viewed the function of the dream as being one of disguise, that is, an attempt to represent the nature of the stimulus as benign rather than important to the dreamer.

In general, Freud thought that the dream serves to conceal that which caused its occurrence. The dream in essence protects the dreamer against the dream instigators. The dream instigators, be they repressed wishes or internal or external stimuli, have the potential to disturb sleep. Hence, by concealing their true nature, the dream preserves the sanctity of sleep.

However, as we now know (chapter 3), dreams are a regularly occurring part of the sleep cycle. As such, it hardly seems likely that they are caused by a fortuitous melding of presleep experiences with repressed infantile wishes as Freud suggested.

It is also clear that stressful or disturbing presleep events are more likely to find their way into our dreams than are benign presleep experiences. This hardly seems

---

*This is often referred to as the "drive discharge" function of dreaming.

in keeping with Freud's idea that benign and stressful daytime experiences play an equivalent role in the production of dream content. In addition, dreams concerned with emotionally disturbing waking experiences are often accompanied by disturbed sleep (chapter 5). This would seem to run counter to Freud's notion that dreams serve to preserve the sanctity of sleep.

Finally, it is apparent that chance events occurring during the night do not instigate dreams as Freud suggested they might. However, both internal somatic conditions (chapter 6) and external events (chapter 7) ostensibly do have the capacity to alter the course of an ongoing dream narrative.

What does all this mean? On the surface, it means quite simply that dreams are sometimes, although not always, in one way or another responsive to a host of forces that impinge on us from time to time. These forces run the gamut from stressful presleep experiences to innocuous events occurring while we are asleep.

So, we're left with some rather important questions to try to answer. Does this responsiveness have any function at all? And, if so, what might this function be?

To try to answer these questions, we'll examine the ideas of some of the theorists who followed Freud. A number of them had the benefit of information provided by contemporary dream research which was of course unavailable to Freud. Most of these theorists would agree that the drive discharge function of dreaming posited by Freud is no longer viable. But as we shall see, strands of Freud's notions, often considerably altered, run through some of the more recent hypotheses concerning the process and function of dreaming advanced by these contemporary theorists.

DREAMS AND THE MASTERY OF STRESS

The fact that stressful waking experiences are more likely to be reflected in or incorporated into dreams led a number of theorists to speculate that dreams may serve to help us deal with or master stressful situations occurring in the course of our daily lives. In this sense they felt that dreams might be adaptive. Dallett[2] called the notions advanced by these theorists "mastery" hypotheses.

While these theories vary in nuance and description of the process of mastery, they all implicitly assume a degree of continuity between our waking and sleeping lives. A number of these theories also suggest that the process of dreaming permits us to tap into memories of past experiences. In this latter sense, it's not unfair to say they are at least somewhat reminiscent of Freudian theory (chapter 2).

For example, according to Louis Breger,[3] the responsiveness of dreams to stressful presleep stimuli is determined by the activation of particular memory systems prior to going to sleep. In his view, emotionally laden presleep events are the ones that have the greatest potential to activate these memory systems. Simply put, stressful waking experiences call up a number of memories of previous, similar, stressful events. When we go to sleep these memory systems spring into action to help formulate our dreams.

A notion such as this is predicated on the idea that the process of dreaming is untrammeled by the restraints associated with waking thought. For one thing, while we sleep, the demands from our external environment with a potential for interruption of the course of problem solution are virtually nonexistent. For another, the solutions we might consider while dreaming are unburdened by concerns for social acceptability. Finally, the process of dreaming seems to permit the free flow of ideas, images and emotions in a manner not possible during the waking state. Presumably this is because the usual restrictions associated with waking thought, such as grammatical constraints or concerns about coherence and the logical form of events, are no longer operative.

So how might this be adaptive? As I mentioned earlier, according to Breger's notion, during the waking state particular memory systems have been readied for action by our emotionally charged waking experiences. When we dream, these memory systems come to the fore. They bring with them not only past similar problems, but also past successful solutions to those problems. Since dreaming is unfettered by the usual constraints associated with waking thought the problems and solutions can be "played" with, they can be tried out, they can be put together in new and creative ways. Because the problem-solving mechanism that is in action while we dream is more fluid and filled with more possibilities than what is generally available to us while we are awake, we are more likely to come up with creative solutions to the waking conflicts which have played an important role in generating our dreams in the first place. To put it another way, dreaming permits present conflicts to be integrated with information about past similar conflicts that have had successful resolutions.

This is not to say that a "solution" to a presleep problem or conflict is automatically presented to the dreamer on waking, as was the case for Kekulé (chapter 1). Rather, according to Breger, the process of integration of the conflicted material might provide a cathartic function, a release of some sort, which enables the dreamer to "awake psychologically 'refreshed' the next morning."[4] A good example of this process may be found in Rosette's dream (chapter 1).

As you'll recall, in the first scene of the dream Rosette's mother is in a turbulent river; she catches a fish and slings it over her back. At the end of the scene, she is pushing "her way through the water with power and concentration." She is going resolutely forward. On her "broad back" she ends up carrying the skeleton of the fish.

In fact, Rosette knew her mother had some skeletons in her closet, skeletons that she was loathe to reveal. She had survived a Nazi concentration camp. But Rosette knew very little about those experiences. According to Rosette, her mother "never initiated any conversation on that subject." Nevertheless, Rosette did know that her mother had successfully plunged ahead through life bearing the weight of those experiences by herself. It could be done.

The second scene of the dream is perhaps somewhat more transparent. Rosette successfully made a difficult landing of her tiny aircraft. She felt "exhilarated and very proud." Rosette is not a pilot. But as she pointed out in her analysis of the dream, she was making a solo flight of sorts in real life. She had recently separated from her husband. She had to go it alone. Within the context of Breger's notion, then, we might speculate that her waking concerns about successfully dealing with life on her own activated memories of previous situations in which she or others had to wade through uncharted waters on their own. It had been done successfully before—by her mother, and no doubt by Rosette as well. So in the final episode of the dream, Rosette was able to experience the pleasure of coming through a difficult and frightening experience unscathed. She had learned how to fly.

In short, Rosette was not left with specific knowledge of how she was going to cope with her situation, but rather, and perhaps more importantly, she was left with the almost somatic understanding that she would be able to cope. Or to put it another way, she would be able to fly on her own.

In this case, obviously, Rosette remembered her dream. However, Breger felt that recall of dreams that integrate a waking stressor with solutions to other similar stressful events is not crucial to the process of mastery. Knowing that we don't remember most of our dreams, he speculated that the "adaptive function [of dreaming] would entail some sort of unconscious mediation between the dream and waking life."[5] In other words, the process of mastery, or at least the feeling associated with mastery, occurring during the dream would be somehow left with us on waking even if we had no conscious awareness of having dreamed.

Obviously such a proposition is not without its drawbacks. One major difficulty is how are we in fact ever going to be able to map the process of mastery? Or to put it another way, how can we demonstrate that mastery has taken place?

A possible line of evidence for the occurrence of mastery, as Breger suggested, might be found in the morning mood of the dreamer. Presumably, those dreamers who have achieved some degree of mastery over anxiety-provoking waking problems, would awaken feeling less anxious than others who had not found solutions to similar problems.

But how could one examine this notion in a meaningful, systematic manner? It's not enough to say, "He was anxious before he went to bed. He woke up in fine fettle. Hence he must have had dreams that helped master the causes of his anxiety." After all, in such a circumstance, it would be just as reasonable to argue that his morning mood was the result of pleasant dreams which made him feel good, rather than the result of dreams that dealt with our dreamer's presleep stress. Evidently, we have to know something about the content of the dreams that transpired during the night.

One promising line of research was an extension of the techniques used to examine the effect of presleep stimuli on dream content (chapter 5). Essentially, the idea was to present subjects with stressful presleep material, take stock of their mood before they went to sleep, collect their dreams during the night and finally measure their mood again in the morning. Presumably, if the subjects were anxious before they went to bed, dreamed about the anxiety-provoking presleep stimulus during the night and were less anxious the following morning, it would be reasonable to speculate that mastery had taken place. In short, incorporation of the presleep event might be viewed as evidence that the process of mastery had been set in motion. The reduction in anxiety in the morning could be taken as evidence that mastery of the stressful presleep event had been successfully completed.

One study using this type of paradigm was done by Cohen and Cox.[6] They placed their subjects in either a negative or positive situation before they went to bed. In a positive situation, the subjects were treated in a friendly fashion and were given easy intellectual tasks to perform before they went to bed. In the negative situation the subjects were treated in a cold and distant manner and were given difficult intellectual tasks to try to complete prior to going to bed. The subjects' moods were measured immediately after they took the tests. Then they were allowed to go to sleep and dreams were collected from their REM periods during the course of the night. Finally, their moods were measured again in the morning.

Among the subjects who had experienced the unpleasant or negative presleep experience, there were indeed some subjects who exhibited an increase in positive mood on waking in the morning. Then Cohen and Cox compared the dream content of these subjects with others from the negative condition who showed no change in mood from night to morning. They found that the subjects whose mood had become more positive were more likely to have dreamed about the anxiety-provoking situation they had experienced before going to bed than subjects whose mood didn't change. Thus, dreaming about the stressful tests seemed to result in a more pleasant mood the following morning, a finding consistent with the mastery hypothesis.

In a study[7] of ours which I mentioned in chapter 5 we used a difficult test as a stressor in much the same manner as Cohen and Cox. On two successive nights we gave one group of subjects a difficult intellectual task, which they could not complete in the allotted time, just before they went to bed. A second group of subjects received a similar, but easy, task to do before going to bed. The first night was a night of uninterrupted sleep. The second was a dream collection night. On both nights we assessed the subjects' mood both before they went to bed and when they awoke in the morning.

After the first night of uninterrupted sleep, we were surprised to discover that both groups of subjects exhibited a reduction in anxiety between the evening and the morning. We were surprised because we expected that only the subjects in the difficult task situation would exhibit such a change. However, we reasoned that even for the subjects in the easy task condition, the experimental situation was itself anxiety provoking and the reduction in anxiety from evening to morning may have reflected successful mastery of this cause of stress.

The dream collection results provided another story altogether. We found that there were some subjects who exhibited an *increase* in anxiety between the evening and the morning. What is more, unlike the results of the Cohen and Cox study, those subjects who showed such an increase also had more incorporations of the presleep experience than those subjects who did not have an evening to morning increase in anxiety. In short, it appeared as if dreaming about the stressful experience, rather than helping to master that event, resulted in more distress on waking.

How can we explain these apparently conflicting results? One way is to say quite simply that at times it is more adaptive to *not* dream about a stressful waking experience than to dream about it. That is, not dreaming about a stressful event may at times result in more pleasant or at least less unpleasant feelings in the morning than dreaming about such an event. I'll discuss this possibility a little later on when we get to the section on avoidance.

But first, let's take a look at a slightly different version of the mastery hypothesis. Greenberg and his colleagues[8] suggested that REM-period dreaming* is adaptive because it permits the integration of emotionally stressful material with an individual's characteristic defenses or coping mechanisms.

---

*In their view it is REM-period dreaming rather than the dreaming that occurs during non-REM sleep that plays a crucial role in adaptation to waking stress.

According to them, in addition to providing a forum for integration the dream also has the task of relegating threatening material to the unconscious. In keeping with this notion, they suggested a completed dream (that is, a dream in which integration has successfully taken place) is a forgotten dream. They also suggested one of the reasons dreams are remembered is because they are unable to adequately defend against threatening material. That is, when the threatening material reaches consciousness because it hasn't been successfully dealt with by characteristic coping mechanisms, the dreamer may be awakened and hence remember the dream.

This idea is interesting for a couple of reasons. For one thing, it is obviously similar to Freud's notion that failed dreams are ones that allow the dreamer to be awakened by threatening material. The main difference of course is in the presumed nature of the threatening material. For Freud the material is likely to be unconscious, repressed wishes. For Greenberg and his colleagues, the threatening material is likely to be a product of some stressful, waking experience.

The other interesting aspect of this notion is that it dovetails nicely with our earlier discussion of dream recall (chapter 8). At that time, we noted it is precisely dreams about disturbing events that are most likely to be remembered. This is because such dreams are often accompanied by brief awakenings. In our view,[9] such awakenings in the midst of the dream enable the dreamer to process the dream in a form compatible with waking thought. This in turn makes it more readily available for future recall during the waking state. One of the logical consequences of this type of processing may be a reduction in the dream's ability to aid in the mastery of contemporary stress.

Why is this so? Let's start with the notion we discussed earlier that during dreaming there is a certain fluidity and flexibility of thought that is not available during the waking state. This flexibility presumably enables the dreamer to combine present events with past successful solutions (Breger) or bring disturbing events under control with characteristic unconscious coping mechanisms (Greenberg and his colleagues). However, when the dreamer is awakened by the dream, this flexibility is no longer available. The disturbing material is again processed in a manner similar to waking thought. Thus instead of multiple tracks of possible solutions to a problem, only a single track of waking thought is now available. In short, the potential for creative problem solution available in the dream may be thwarted because the dream is robbed of its characteristic fluidity and flexibility of thought and emotion. Consequently, on the basis of the information we have about dream recall, it seems reasonable to speculate that the dreams most fruitful in the process of mastery will be those that are not remembered. This is because it is during those dreams that fluidity of thought and emotion will be best able to be maintained.

In any case, working on the assumption that dreams do aid in the mastery of contemporary stress, Greenberg and his colleagues decided to explore the consequences of taking an individual's dreams away. They decided to use a REM deprivation procedure similar to those I described earlier (chapter 9). While most other studies concentrated on the ability of subjects to perform specific tasks after REM deprivation, Greenberg and his colleagues were particularly interested in possible changes in the psychological responses of their subjects after such deprivation. They in fact had the expectation that REM deprivation might have some deleterious consequences.

Accordingly, they embarked on a series of REM deprivation experiments to explore this possibility. In the first of these studies[10] they merely attempted to examine cognitive and emotional functioning after REM deprivation. To do this, they compared their subjects' performances on a number of different types of tasks. They were able to demonstrate that while REM deprivation had no effect on cognitive performance (tests of learning, memory and so forth) or vigilance, it did have consequences for emotional responses on various projective tests. As they put it, ". . . with dream deprivation, *feelings* and *wishes* which have been kept out of consciousness now appear more overtly in the test protocols of all four subjects."[11]

Why did this happen? Greenberg and his colleagues speculated that in the course of their daily lives during the experiment, the subjects probably had a number of waking experiences that activated unconscious unresolved conflicts. According to them, under normal conditions such conflicts would have been dealt with in a temporary fashion in the waking state. For example, they could have been put aside or suppressed for a limited time. Ultimately, however, dreaming would have provided the means for the successful integration of the threatening material with existing defense mechanisms and relegated the material to the unconscious. But, of course, in this experiment the subjects were prevented from dreaming, or at least from having REM-period dreams. As a consequence, they did not have the opportunity to defend against the threatening material in their characteristic fashions and as a result the unconscious wishes and feelings spilled over into waking life.

Greenberg and his colleagues suggested that one of the benefits of integration of threatening waking material with existing mechanisms of defense would be to make it easier to deal with similar events in the future. In other words, they believed that future encounters with a similar stressful experience would be more readily handled in waking life after such an integration had taken place. Their subsequent REM deprivation experiments were designed to explore this possibility.

In one study,[12] Greenberg and his collaborators selected subjects who were especially likely to become emotionally involved in a particular presleep task. They expected these subjects to feel threatened if they were unable to complete the task. Accordingly, before going to bed, the subjects were given a series of anagrams to solve.

The task was designed so that approximately half of the anagrams could be solved in the forty-five seconds allotted for each one. There were a number of groups in this study, but for our purposes we need be concerned with only two of them. One group of subjects was REM deprived. Another group was awakened the same number of times as the REM deprived group, but their awakenings occurred during non-REM sleep.

There was no difference between the two groups in their ability to recall successfully completed anagrams the next morning. However, the REM deprived subjects remembered fewer incomplete anagrams than their counterparts who had been awakened during non-REM sleep. In other words, the subjects who were allowed to have REM-period dreams were better able to cope with the threatening consequences of remembering tasks they had failed than those who had been prevented from having such dreams. Greenberg and his colleagues interpreted these results as a demonstration that dreaming aided in the integration of the "current stressful experience with similar experiences from the past through the use of customary coping mechanisms."[13] They argued that once such integration had taken place, there was no longer any need for the subjects to repress* the unpleasant memory of the failed tasks.

In another study,[14] Greenberg and his colleagues showed their subjects a disturbing film about autopsies before they went to bed. They were shown the same film again the next morning. In the interim, half of the subjects were REM deprived and half of the subjects were awakened during non-REM sleep. Based on their notion of the integrative capacities of dreaming, Greenberg and his col-

---

*According to Freud we have a number of mechanisms available to us with which to defend against or deny unwanted information. One of these mechanisms is repression—the exclusion of unwanted information from consciousness (chapter 8).

leagues believed that the subjects permitted to have REM sleep would deal with the stresses induced by the autopsy film with their characteristic defense mechanisms. As a result, they reasoned, those subjects would be better able to handle the film the second time around than would the REM deprived group. Presumably, this latter group would not have had the opportunity to bring their defense mechanisms to bear on the threatening material. As expected, on the second viewing the REM deprived subjects were less able to cope with the autopsy film than the subjects who were awakened only during non-REM sleep.

Unfortunately, one of the problems associated with the studies I've just described is that we have no information about the dream content of the subjects who were awakened during non-REM sleep. Within the general context of the mastery notions we've discussed, we would expect that the subjects awakened only during non-REM sleep had an opportunity to dream of the stressful or threatening presleep events during REM sleep. Presumably, the incorporation of the stressful experiences into their dreams enabled the subjects to successfully deal with those events in one fashion or another.

To examine this possibility, we[15] undertook a study that attempted to test the mastery notion but permitted us to gather dreams. Like Greenberg and his colleagues we showed our subjects a stressful film* prior to their bedtime and again in the morning. However, instead of REM depriving our subjects, we awakened them in the midst of their REM periods and collected their dreams. On the basis of the mastery notion we expected that subjects who dreamed about the film would be less disturbed on viewing it a second time than subjects who didn't dream about it. But as Robert Burns wrote, "The best layed schemes o' mice and men gan aft a-gley."

---

*The film we chose was a workman's compensation film depicting a series of workshop accidents which I described earlier (chapter 7).

Contrary to our expectations, subjects who dreamed about the film during the night were more disturbed on viewing it the second time than subjects who did not. What is more, another group of subjects who viewed the film twice with an eight-hour waking interval also tended to be more anxious on the second viewing. In other words, the response of the subjects who dreamed about the film was similar to that of the subjects who had a chance to think about the film while awake.

Could it be that *not* dreaming about a stressful waking event is somehow more adaptive than dreaming about it? Or to put it another way, might dreaming about something other than a contemporary stressful situation be potentially useful or helpful to the dreamer? A good starting point for looking at this question might be to consider the role of dreams in relation to Jung's notion of compensation.[16]

DREAMS AND COMPENSATION

In Jung's view, our psyche, or self if you will, consists of both conscious and unconscious components. Both of these components are always present, but we are generally unaware of the ongoing, unconscious activity during our waking lives. However, from time to time we are presented with evidence of this unconscious energy. Jung wrote, "Not a day passes but we make some slip of the tongue, or something slips our memory which at other times we know perfectly well, or we are seized by a mood which we cannot trace, etc. These things are all symptoms of some consistent unconscious activity which becomes directly visible at night in dreams, but only occasionally breaks through the inhibitions imposed by our daytime consciousness."[17]

Jung felt that these unconscious processes stand in a complementary or compensatory relationship to our conscious functioning. As he put it,

> The psyche is a self-regulating system that maintains itself in equilibrium as the body does. Every process that goes too far immediately and inevitably calls forth a compensatory activity. Without such adjustments a normal metabolism would not exist, nor would a normal psyche. We can take the idea of compensation, so understood, as a law of psychic happening. Too little on one side results in too much on the other. The relationship between conscious and unconscious is compensatory.[18]

In other words, according to Jung, compensation is a constant, ongoing process. It involves an interplay of the conscious and unconscious. But as he suggested, while we are awake we are generally not privy to the other part of ourselves which is the unconscious and hence we're not aware of this compensatory activity. However, when we sleep and dream, our unconscious comes to the fore and it is then that we are more likely to find evidence of compensation.

There are a few studies that are often cited as evidence of the existence of compensatory dreams. For example, in one study,[19] five volunteers were kept in social isolation during the course of the day. Their dreams the following night contained a substantial number of instances of social interactions. In other words, the dreams of the subjects seemed to make up or compensate for the lack of social contacts they had during the day. These results seem to fit quite nicely and directly into the mold of the compensatory theory of dreaming.

In another study I described earlier (chapter 6), Hauri[20] found that subjects dreamed less about the activity they had engaged in extensively before going to sleep. As you'll recall, in that study subjects who engaged in intellectual activity before bedtime had less dream content related to thinking or problem-solving during the night. However, when the same subjects went to bed after strenuous physical activity, they tended to dream more about sitting around or thinking.

In still another study,[21] the dreams of young boys were collected after they viewed a Western film on one night and a baseball documentary on another. The Western film contained aggressive action, while the baseball film contained no violence or aggression. The dreams following the baseball film were more hostile and frightening than were the dreams following the Western film. Within the compensatory model we might interpret these results as demonstrating that the unconscious was supplying the aspects of aggression and hostility that were missing from conscious waking experience. Or alternatively we could speculate that the dreams following the Western film were more benign as the result of unconscious compensation for the violence in the presleep experience.

Now returning to our own film study, which I described in the last section, we are presented with a problem. We have to ask ourselves if in that situation not dreaming about the stressful presleep film constituted compensation. Or to put it in a general way, can *not* dreaming about a disturbing experience be construed as a compensatory act?

It appears to me the answer to this question is probably not. Including "not dreaming" about an event under the heading of compensation really seems to be stretching things. Well if that's the case, what should we call it? And what function if any does not dreaming about waking stressful events have for the dreamer? For want of a better term, I think not dreaming about disturbing or threatening experiences fits under the category of "avoidance."* What's more, I think avoidance does have a function which is itself adaptive in nature.[22]

---

*Indeed, as we'll see a bit later on, it's probably most useful and meaningful to consider compensatory dreams as just a particular form of avoidance dreams.

DREAMS AND AVOIDANCE

To begin with, it's important to keep in mind a point I made earlier in this chapter. Dreams seem to be responsive to the things that go on around us. In this sense, although it may be a heresy, I think it's safe to say that dreams are no different than waking thoughts.

For example, let's say I took you to the zoo and introduced you to a huge, green, very friendly elephant named Henrietta. You would in all likelihood think of this unusual creature at various times later that day when you had some moments to yourself. You might even conjure up images of Henrietta. You might even think of her from time to time later in the week.

But what if you had something important to do like study for an exam? Or what if you were engrossed in some activity like reading a compelling novel or concentrating on your next move in a game of chess you were playing by mail with your friend in Istanbul? My guess is that under those circumstances you would probably push thoughts of Henrietta aside and get down to the task at hand.

At night, as you drifted off to sleep, perhaps your mind would again wander to the delightful Henrietta. Your dreams might well be filled with pleasant images, your breathing regular, your brief awakenings few in number. As Keats put it:

A thing of beauty is a joy forever
Its loveliness·increases; it will never
Pass into nothingness; but still will keep
A bower quiet for us, and a sleep
Full of sweet dreams, and health, and
      quiet breathing.

Up to now, Henrietta was an ordinary, run of the mill, huge, but very pleasant, green elephant. Now let's make her a bit nasty. Let's say I didn't introduce her to you in the zoo. Rather let's imagine that you came upon her suddenly in a dark alley late at night. She loomed above you, an ugly luminescent green in the washed-out light from a nearby street lamp. Rather than greeting you with a polite hello as she had in the zoo scenario, she bellowed at you in a gravelly, menacing voice, "Your money or your life."

You felt the sweat starting to pour from your body. With trembling hands you reached into your pockets, pulled out your money and placed it in the horny folds of her twisted trunk. "Is that all of it?"she growled.

"Yes, sir."

"I'm not a sir," she shouted angrily.

"Sorry, ma'am," you squeaked in a thoroughly frightened voice, "that's all the money I have."

"Well then, get the hell out of here," Henrietta yelled.

You turned around and ran as fast as you could. You ran until you could run no more. Shaking, you leaned against a parked car to catch your breath. Finally, you reached home. Once inside, you slammed the door shut, double locked it and pushed a chest of drawers against it. Only then were you able to sit down with an almost inaudible sigh of relief.

Now if you tried to get Henrietta out of your mind it wouldn't be a simple matter. My guess is she wouldn't be just an idle thought when you had nothing on your mind. Chances are she would dominate your thoughts. You'd have difficulty concentrating on anything else. As you tried to study for your upcoming exams images of the menacing Henrietta would constantly intrude on your mind. Try as you might, you'd find it almost impossible to push her from your mind. You'd probably spend most of your waking hours trying to deal with your frightening experience. When you went to bed, if you could fall asleep, you would almost surely have disturbing dreams about your encounter with Henrietta. Your accompanying sleep would no doubt be punctuated by a number of awakenings and perhaps by increased heart and respiratory rates. As Shakespeare so aptly put it:

Nature seems dead; and wicked dreams
   abuse
The curtain'd sleep. . . .

In short, as we discussed earlier your dreams would likely reflect your waking concerns. In this case it would be the fear brought on by the traumatic encounter with Henrietta. As a result your sleep would no doubt suffer as well.

The Nature and Function of Avoidance Dreams

As the days and weeks passed, you would begin to come to grips with your traumatic experience. The way you did so would depend on your particular psychological makeup. For example, maybe you'd be able to rid yourself of the fear by telling yourself such an experience could never happen again. After all, how many large, green hostile elephants are running around loose in this world?

Whatever tack you took, as time went on we can be sure that your experience with Henrietta would prey less and less on your mind. In addition, while awake, the demands of your life would help push the traumatic incident from your thoughts.

Your dreams would also reflect the lessened importance of the unhappy experience in your life. However, because there are none of the usual external diversions while you sleep, Henrietta might still rear her ugly trunk while you dream. And again, your sleep might be subject to disturbance. It is here that avoidance dreams would come into play.

Avoidance dreams help to preserve the integrity of sleep. We know from sleep deprivation studies (chapter 9) that there is a need for the sleeper to obtain his or her normal complement of sleep. Avoidance dreams enable sleep to continue in a relatively normal or undisturbed manner precisely by *avoiding* grappling with stressful material in a potentially sleep-disturbing manner.

The form of avoidance dreams no doubt varies from individual to individual. For example, you might have *compensatory* dreams in which you are chasing a huge, green elephant rather than the other way around. Or you may have dreams in which the elephant appears but you are not fearful. This would be similar to some of the dreams of our phobic subject[23] (chapter 5). During the course of desensitization he occasionally dreamed of material related to his phobias without the usual accompanying anxiety. Or finally you simply may *not* dream about the unpleasant incident at all. In its place may be an entirely different, benign experience.

Up to now, we've been discussing avoidance dreams in relation to waking experiences. However, some dreams that respond to ongoing somatic conditions or external events may also be considered avoidance dreams. I'm referring specifically to those dreams that serve to disguise the nature of an internal or external stimulus in such a manner as to permit the dreamer to continue sleeping.

For instance, what Freud called "dreams of convenience" (chapter 2) might be subsumed under avoidance dreams. As an example, let's say you became thirsty during the night. You dreamed of drinking a cold beer. As a result you avoided the implications of being thirsty. You didn't need to wake up to get a drink as Freud did. You were able to stay asleep. In this instance we might reasonably argue that the dream successfully prevented you from being awakened by a disturbing somatic stimulus.*

Similarly, as we saw in chapter 7, those dreams that are able to rob an external event of its potentially disturb-

---

*It's interesting to note that some of Bokert's water-deprived subjects (chapter 6) who dreamed about quenching their thirst during the night actually reported being less thirsty the next morning!

ing aspects also serve an avoidance function. For example, it is possible that you would be able to sleep through a
noisy thunderstorm if the claps of thunder were incorporated into an ongoing dream as the noise accompanying a particularly brilliant display of fireworks. In this example, just as with the somatic stimulus, the dream
would have enabled you to continue sleeping.

Admittedly, these latter types of avoidance dreams
are not likely to be frequently occurring events. They are
more or less fortuitous in nature. For one thing, as we
discussed earlier, you would almost surely have had to be
in the process of dreaming when the events occurred. For
another, your dream probably would have to have an existing context that would permit the incorporation of the
potentially disturbing stimulus in a relatively benign
fashion. And finally, as we've already mentioned, if the
somatic or external stimuli continued to persist, you'd
very likely be awakened anyway. In short, it's probably
safe to say avoidance dreams are most important in protecting sleep from the potentially disturbing effects of
stressful presleep experiences.

Insofar as avoidance dreams help to preserve the integrity of sleep, they are undoubtedly adaptive. But they
may also contribute to the sense of well-being on waking
that Breger attributed only to successful mastery dreams.
Probably they do so in two ways. First of all, it seems
reasonable to think that having a good night's sleep helps
us to feel well in the morning. We wake up refreshed,
ready to tackle the events of the coming day. Second,
there is some evidence suggesting morning mood is
related to dream content.[24] If this is indeed the case, it's
not unreasonable to speculate that avoidance dreams that
are pleasant in tone may result in a good feeling on awak-
ing in the morning.

"Wait a second," you might say. "This is all well and
good, but what about all the other studies we've discussed
up to now? You know, the ones that showed we often
dream in a rather direct, undisguised manner about

troublesome waking events. Clearly, those dreams are not avoidance dreams. In fact, a mastery explanation of those types of dreams seems pretty reasonable to me. Are you now trying to tell me to forget about the mastery notions altogether? Are you suggesting that the only adaptive function dreams may have is to provide a respite from unhappy events? Are you suggesting the avoidance explanation for dreaming is 'better' than the mastery explanation?''

The answer to all of your questions is an unequivocal, emphatic "no!" As far as I can tell, there is no reason to think dreams have only one particular function. In fact, Janet Wright and I suggested that dreams may function in both mastery and avoidance capacities, albeit at different times.[25]

DISRUPTION AND AVOIDANCE

Let's return to my original suggestion that dreams may function in a manner similar to waking thoughts. While we are awake, if we are confronted by a disturbing event or important problem, we have a hard time pushing it out of our minds. Nonetheless, from time to time we are able to push such concerns aside. Some of the time we do so because the demands of waking life force us to concentrate on business at hand. Other times we do so because we've had enough. We need a break from these harsher aspects of our lives.

Over the long haul, these concerns will keep cropping up until we've successfully dealt with them. Dealing with them can at times mean finding actual solutions to concrete problems. But more often than not it means handling them psychologically, dealing with them so they no longer plague us. In short it means putting them aside in one way or another so that we can get on with our lives. Attempts to handle or deal with our problems probably begin around the time a stressful event occurs during the waking state.

The form of the resolution, as well as the time it takes for it to occur, is no doubt dependent on both the nature of the individual experiencing the stress and the type of problem confronting him or her. Some people can turn the simplest problems into momentous ones, and take forever to deal with them. Others can deal with seemingly major crises in surprisingly quick and efficient ways. Finally, of course, there are certain problems or concerns that apparently are never fully dealt with. They evidently can be pushed aside or temporarily put out of our minds. But they may crop up from time to time in spite of ourselves with resulting consequences for our dreams and sleep. The war experiences of both veterans and refugees we discussed in chapter 5 are good examples of this type of profound concern.

If our waking attempts at mastery have not been completely successful, our concerns are likely to reappear again in our dreams. This is particularly true because during sleep we are not confronted by other demands which generally mark our daily lives. We are free, as it were, to concentrate on our ongoing problems. But as we have seen, dreaming about disturbing events is not without its drawbacks. Our sleep patterns may well be altered. Our disturbing dreams may awaken us. Generally the awakenings are brief. But they can be longer. Occasionally we may even be kept awake for a lengthy period of time by the memories of a disturbing dream we just had. In short, dreaming about our problems can disrupt our sleep.

How can we cope with these disturbing dreams? Aside from staying awake all night, which hardly seems like a good solution, our only recourse is to somehow rid ourselves of such dreams. But we have a problem. Dreams occur like clockwork during the night. We can't just "turn them off." Consequently the only strategy we have available to us is to somehow supplant the disturbing dreams with pleasant ones. That's where avoidance dreams come in.

Based on the evidence I described up to now, we[26] suggested that when we are confronted by a disturbing waking experience it has the potential to disturb sleep. The extent to which this potential will be realized is dependent on a number of things. For example, it depends on how disturbing the waking experience is to us.* It also depends on how able we are to cope with the disturbing experience while we are still awake. If we can effectively deal with a stressful event while we're awake, it is less likely to disturb us after we go to sleep. On the other hand, if we have not successfully dealt with the event, it is likely to intrude on our dreams.

In our view, dreaming about the disturbing experience represents an attempt at mastery. But since, as we have seen, attempts at mastery are often accompanied by a disruption in sleep, from time to time avoidance dreams would come to the fore, thus helping to preserve the normal pattern and integrity of sleep. Avoidance dreams may occur on the same night as disruptive dreams. Or they may take place on subsequent nights. But in any case, we expect that the interplay between mastery and avoidance dreams would continue until some sort of psychological resolution of the focal problem came about.

Of course the big question as always is, can we demonstrate that there is an oscillation or interplay between mastery and avoidance dreams? And indeed, there are a couple of studies that seem to indicate that such an oscillation does take place.

In one study,[27] after an adaptation night, dreams were collected from REM periods during a baseline night. On subsequent nights subjects were shown either a neutral, documentary film or one of two stressful films

---

*Obviously, the same experience may be more disturbing to one person than to another (chapter 5).

just before bedtime. Some subjects saw the neutral film first and others viewed the stressful film first. Dreams were collected from the REM periods of these nights as well.

A number of different physiological measures were taken on each of the subjects before and after viewing both films. As you might expect, there were no differences in these measures when subjects viewed the neutral film. The response to the stressful film was a different matter. Two subjects were labeled strong responders, that is, they were extremely affected by viewing the stressful film. Four subjects exhibited a limited response to the stressful film, and one subject exhibited no response at all. Obviously this is still another instance of different people being affected to a greater or lesser degree by the same experience.

The dreams that were collected from the first and last REM periods of the night following the neutral film were essentially no different from those collected from the same REM periods on the baseline night. However, following the stressful film, the dreams of the first REM period were generally more anxious and aggressive, while dreams of the last REM period of the night were no different in mood than the dreams from the last REM period following the neutral film. What is more, some of the subjects exhibited incorporation of the film in the first dreams of the night while others had such incorporations in the last dream of the night. Those having the early incorporations exhibited a greater decrease in anxiety and aggression in their last dreams than subjects who incorporated the stressful film into their last dreams.

The authors interpreted these results as indicating that both mastery and compensation had taken place, and they both are "equally effective in working through the impact of the disturbing movies."[28]

However, in the context of our discussion up to now, I think there is a simpler and more straightforward explanation of these results. It goes something like this: Subjects were affected differently by the stressful films. Each of the subjects had his own particular style of dealing with the stress, both before falling asleep and while dreaming. The differences in the dream content reflect these differences in style. Some subjects began the night by dreaming openly about the stressful event. These dreams probably represent attempts to master or deal with the stressful experience. As so often happens with mastery dreams, they were accompanied by disturbing emotions. Later dreams, containing no incorporations, fit in the category of avoidance dreams. Such avoidance dreams could have occurred because the attempts at mastery had been successful and hence there was no need to dream about the stressful event anymore. Or they could have taken place because the dreamer wished to push potentially disturbing material from his mind in order to maintain the sanctity of sleep.

On the other hand, some subjects started the night with avoidance dreams. As a result there was no opportunity for mastery to take place. Consequently, when these subjects finally got around to dreaming about the disturbing presleep experience, their dreams were accompanied by the unpleasant emotions associated with their presleep experience. Evidently, in these cases attempts to master the stressful experience had been held in abeyance until the night's end.

The results of this study seem to indicate that both avoidance dreams and mastery dreams can occur on a single night following a stressful experience. However, the order or pattern of occurrence of these dreams probably depends on a couple of things. First, it probably depends on the potency the stressor holds for a particular individual. And second, it probably depends on each individual's characteristic style of coping with stressful situations.

But one thing this study can't tell us is whether the mastery process was successfully completed. If it was, we would expect to see no evidence of the stressful film in dreams on subsequent nights, or at least no evidence of the stressful film accompanied by anxiety or aggression. However, if mastery was not attained either during dreaming or later during the waking state, we would expect to see film elements and a concomitant disturbed mood in dreams of future nights. A study[29] of our own which I described earlier (chapter 5) has some bearing on this issue.

In that home dream study, we collected dreams from eight consecutive nights. Prior to the third night we gave our subjects either a difficult or easy test to work on. What follows are the transcriptions of the dreams of one subject. They are collected from the first, third and sixth nights after he had taken the difficult test.

Here is the dream from the first post-test night:

What I have just finished dreaming about is . . . the aptitude test, believe it or not. The idea was . . . that . . . I had not done so well. And it just so happened that I was taken away, for further analysis you might say. And . . . apparently they discovered I needed some, care. . . . As it turned out, I ended up in . . . the ah, mental hospital I guess you could call it. I did not like this situation to say the least. It ah was pretty ah typical of what you might imagine. There was not a lot of color. It was mostly white with ah everybody being dressed in white as well. The situation was bleak and ah it seemed as if I was being sentenced to a prison term, because there was something the matter with me. I don't believe that at all but that's what happened in my dream. Ah, all I can say is that I hope . . . this is not the case at all. My emotions in the dream were mainly that of being scared, confused . . . and as I said before, there were no vivid colors. It was mainly white. I seemed to be making a lot of noise while everybody else around me seemed rather passive. . . . It seemed as if I was fighting for my life, because I could not believe what exactly was happening to me. That's about all I can say about the dream. Oh, I felt cold clammy sweat.

Next comes the dream from the third post-test night:

> Ah, I just had a dream which I've had many times before. It seems more like a nightmare than a dream. It's not pleasant at all. . . . It is one with no definite purpose. I'm given an impossible task. Something that there's no way that can be done by me for who- ever it is that ah has given me the task. It seems like . . . it is an assignment . . . given to me, and there's no way that I can do it. There's no definite scene it seems. . . . And, it, to say the least, is a very strange dream. You could call it a nightmare I suppose. It borders on a nightmare. . . . As I said, there, I'm given a task in which I'm not sure which it is. There's no way to do it in the time that I have allotted to do it. And it seems that something bad will happen if I do not complete the task. Of course in this case I am very scared. I . . . don't know what it is that I've been given to do. . . . This task had to be done or something very bad was going to happen to me such as ah torture . . . punishment, and maybe even death. It was not very pleasant. Ah . . . the job that I was given to do, I was required to do it alone, in the allotted time. . . . but as I said, I cannot give you a description of what I was to do . . . and that's about all I can say really.

Finally we have the dream from the sixth post-test night:

> I have just had a very pleasant dream. . . . Um, my brother and I were going down the highway and I sup- pose our destination would have been Detroit or the area of Detroit, Windsor mainly I suppose ah he and I are planning on going down to Windsor and Detroit for a week or so before the University starts once again in September. And the dream which I just had

. . . um, we are on the highway . . . and we are just cruising around sixty miles per hour. Huh, he is driving his car. The colors are very vivid. The sky is clear. The grass is green. The trees are green. Typical colors you know but they are all very vivid. Hm . . . we are just ah cruising along down the highway, listening to the stereo, tape or radio or whatever it happened to be. However it seems that I can't remember what song it was that was playing. However, it seemed to be very suitable for our situation, if you know what I mean. Ah . . . in the dream I was very relaxed in the car, very happy. Ah . . . the ride was smooth I guess you could say. Ah . . . we weren't talking too much. Just taking in the scenery, listening to the music. We were both very happy. He seemed to have a smile on his face. I was very relaxed but rather anxious to get where we were going. And . . . so was he I suppose. It seemed there weren't many cars on the highway. It seemed to be in the afternoon in the summer. We were alone as a matter of fact, looking back. We were yeah definitely the only car on the highway. . . . That's about all I can remember.

So what we have is the highly charged, unpleasant emotional experience of an uncompleted task appearing as a central theme in a dream on the night following the actual test experience. The dream is obviously accompanied by a great deal of anxiety. What's more, it appeared again, in an almost identical form in a dream three nights later. And again it was accompanied by feelings of anxiety. It is only on the sixth night after the test that the reported dream is a pleasant one. At last the dreamer has extricated himself from the testing situation as he and his brother drive happily (away from the university).

This sequence of dreams is similar to a pattern we observed in many of our subjects. The most frequent dreams about the testing experience occurred on the night immediately following the test, and again on the third, fourth and fifth nights after the test. On the second night and again on the sixth night there was a drop in the number of subjects who reported dreaming about the test.

Why did this pattern emerge? Let's look at it within the context of the disruption-avoidance notion. In an attempt to master or deal with the stressful experience on the night immediately following the testing, our subjects dreamed overtly about the stressor. Presumably these dreams led to a disruption in sleep.* In response to this disruption, the next night was marked by avoidance dreams which helped to preserve normal sleep patterns. But concerns about the test experience obviously did not just disappear. Quite the contrary, they resurfaced in dreams on the next three nights, only to recede again on the sixth night.

One other point worth noting. We asked our subjects to give us an indication of how they felt on waking each morning. We were particularly interested in what might be called unpleasant emotions—aggression, anxiety, depression and distrust. In general, there was more unpleasant feeling following nights in which there had been incorporation of the test experience. Or to look at it from another perspective, not dreaming about the stressful event seemed to have the added beneficial effect of reducing the amount of unpleasant feeling on waking in the morning.

Interestingly, the film study I described earlier and this last study are almost complementary in nature. The former, laboratory, study involved dream collection from more than one REM period on a single night following a

---

*Because this was a home dream study we were unable to record the sleep patterns of these subjects. However, as I've mentioned before and as we've seen in chapter 5, dreaming about disturbing presleep events often does result in changes in sleep patterns including an increase in the number of brief awakenings during the night.

stressful experience. The latter, home dream collection study, involved the collection of dreams over a period of several nights. Taken together they provide some evidence that dreams containing elements of stressful presleep events can be interspersed with dreams of avoidance. These different types of dreams can occur within a single night as well as over the course of several nights following a stressful waking event.

A SUMMING UP

Each night when we go to sleep, we can look forward to having a number of dreams. Their duration will increase as the night progresses. The nature of their content will often reflect our waking experiences as seen through the filters of our own, individual personalities.

As we prepare for sleep, events or concerns that are of importance to us are likely to surge forward into consciousness. No longer hampered by demands or distractions typically associated with our waking lives, we can turn our attention to circumstances we were forced to push aside during the day. These last thoughts before falling asleep are in turn likely to find their way into our dreams. Some of these dreams, usually the last dream of a given night, will be remembered. Most will be forgotten.

Remembered or not, our dreams may still be of benefit to us. They may well serve some adaptive functions. Based on our discussion up to now, we can at least make some interesting speculations about what those adaptive functions might be.

Insofar as dreams reflect waking experience, they may help us to deal with stressful or troublesome waking events. During dreaming, there is a flexibility and fluidity of thought and emotion not generally available during our waking lives. Such plasticity may provide an invaluable aid to finding solutions to our problems or at least to learning how to cope with them.

Dreams may also be useful in helping to preserve the sanctity of sleep. Insofar as dream content does not reflect presleep stress, insofar as it is pleasant or at least neutral in tone, dreams may help us to avoid unwanted, potentially disruptive alterations of the normal pattern of sleep. To a lesser extent, dreams may also help to preserve sleep from intrusions of transient somatic or external events that may occur from time to time. By robbing such stimuli of their significance they may enable the dreamer to continue sleeping.

Whether these speculations fall by the wayside or prove to be correct awaits the test of time. Indeed there may well be other functions of dreaming that we haven't even thought of as yet. Far from being over, the study of dreams which seems to have been going on forever may in fact just be in its infancy.

NOTES

Chapter 1. Sleeping and Dreaming

1. Kleitman, N. (1963) *Sleep and wakefulness* (2nd ed.). Chicago: University of Chicago Press.

2. Lavie, P. and Hobson, J. A. (1986) Origin of dreams: Anticipation of modern theories in the philosophy and physiology of the eighteenth and nineteenth centuries. *Psychological Bulletin, 100*, 229–240.

3. Hadfield, J. A. (1954) *Dreams and nightmares.* Middlesex: Penguin Books Ltd.

4. Freud, S. (1965) *The interpretation of dreams.* (J. Strachey, trans.) New York: Avon. (Originally published, 1900.)

5. Lavie and Hobson, Origin of dreams: Anticipation of modern theories in the philosophy and physiology of the eighteenth and nineteenth centuries.

6. Malcolm, N. (1959) *Dreaming.* London: Routledge & Kegan Paul Ltd.

7. Bartlett, F. C. (1932) *Remembering.* Cambridge, England: Cambridge University Press.

Chapter 2. Freud and Dreaming

1. Freud, S. (1965) *The interpretation of dreams.* (J. Strachey, trans.) New York: Avon, p. 435 (Originally published, 1900.)

2. Jones, R. M. (1970) *The new psychology of dreaming.* New York: Grune & Stratton, Inc.

3. Ibid.

4. Breger, L. (1967) Function of dreams. *Journal of Abnormal Psychology, 72* (Monograph No. 5, Whole No. 641), 1–28.

5. Freud, *The interpretation of dreams*, p. 140.

6. Ibid., p. 151.

7. Freud, S. (1959) Metapsychological supplement to the theory of dreams. (C. M. Baines, trans.) In E. Jones (Ed.) *Sigmund Freud, Collected Papers*, V. 4, New York: Basic Books, pp. 137–138.

8. Freud, *The interpretation of dreams*, p. 609.

9. Ibid., p. 267.

10. Ibid., p. 606.

11. Ibid., p. 590.

12. Ibid., pp. 156–157.

13. Maury, L. F. A. (1861) *Le someil et les rêves.* Paris: Didier and Co.

14. Freud, *The Interpretation of dreams*, p. 591.

15. Ibid., pp. 599–600.

16. Ibid., p. 530.

17. Ibid., p. 607.

18. Dallett, J. (1973) Theories of dream function. *Psychological Bulletin, 79*, 408–416.

Chapter 3. Sleep and Dream Research

1. Koulack, D. (1969) Effects of somatosensory stimulation on dream content. *Archives of General Psychiatry, 20*, p. 721.

2. Aserinsky, E. and Kleitman, N. (1953) Regularly occurring periods of eye motility, and concomitant phenomena, dur-

ing sleep. *Science, 118,* 273–274. See also Aserinsky, E. and Kleitman, N. (1955) Two types of ocular motility in sleep. *Journal of Applied Physiology, 8,* 1–10.

3. Kleitman, N. (1963) *Sleep and wakefulness.* (2nd ed.) Chicago: University of Chicago Press, p. 94.

4. Ladd, G. T. (1892) Contribution to the psychology of visual imagery in dreams. *Mind, 1,* 299–304.

5. Dement, W. (1955) Dream recall and eye movements during sleep in schizophrenics and normals. *Journal of Nervous and Mental Disease, 122,* 263–269. See also Dement, W. and Kleitman, N. (1957) The relation of eye movements during sleep to dream activity: An objective method for the study of dreaming. *Journal of Experimental Psychology, 53,* 339–346.

6. *Webster's New Twentieth Century Dictionary* (1977) (2nd Edition). U.S.A.: William Collins + World Publishing Co., Inc., p. 1527.

7. Dement, W. and Kleitman, N. (1957) Cyclic variations in EEG during sleep and their relation to eye movements, body motility and dreaming; *Electroencephalography and Clinical Neurophysiology, 9,* 673–690.

8. Malcolm, N. (1962) *Dreaming.* London: Routledge & Kegan Paul Ltd.

9. Dement, W. C. and Wolpert, E. A. (1958) The relation of eye movements, body motility, and external stimuli to dream content. *Journal of Experimental Psychology, 55,* p. 550.

10. Koulack, D. (1968) Dream time and real time. *Psychonomic Science, 11,* 202.

11. Ibid., p. 202.

12. Koulack, Effects of somatosensory stimulation on dream content. p. 721.

13. Webb, W. B. and Kersey, J. (1967) Recall of dreams and the probability of stage-1 REM sleep. *Perceptual and Motor Skills, 24,* 627–630.

Chapter 4. Explorations of Dreaming

1. Dement, W. and Kleitman, N. (1957) Cyclic variations in EEG during sleep and their relation to eye movements, body motility and dreaming; *Electroencephalography and Clinical Neurophysiology, 9,* 673–690.

2. Goodenough, D. R., Shapiro, A., Holden, M. and Steinschriber, L. A. (1959) A comparison of "dreamers" and "nondreamers": Eye movements, electroencephalograms, and the recall of dreams. *Journal of Abnormal and Social Psychology, 59,* 295–302. And Foulkes, D. (1962) Dream reports from different stages of sleep. *Journal of Abnormal and Social Psychology, 65,* 14–25.

3. Foulkes, Dream reports from different stages of sleep.

4. Rechtschaffen, A., Verdone, P. and Wheaton, J. (1963) Reports of mental activity during sleep. *Canadian Psychiatric Association Journal, 8,* p. 411.

5. Monroe, L. J., Rechtschaffen, A., Foulkes, D. and Jensen, J. (1965) Discriminability of REM and NREM reports. *Journal of Personality and Social Psychology, 2,* 456–460.

6. Antrobus, J. S., Antrobus, J. S. and Fisher, C. (1965) Discrimination of dreaming and nondreaming sleep. *Archives of General Psychiatry, 12,* 395–401.

7. LaBerge, S., Levitan, L., Gordon, M. and Dement, W. C. (1983) Physiological characteristics of three types of lucid dreams. Paper presented at the 4th International Congress of Sleep Research, Bologna, Italy.

8. Vaughn, C. J. (1964) *The development and use of an operant conditioning technique to provide evidence for visual imagery in the Rhesus monkey under sensory deprivation.* Unpublished Doctoral Dissertation, University of Pittsburgh.

9. Dement, W. and Kleitman, N. (1957) The relation of eye movements during sleep to dream activity: An objective method for the study of dreaming. *Journal of Experimental Psychology, 53,* p. 344.

10. Roffwarg, H. P., Dement, W. C., Muzio, J. N. and Fisher, C. (1962) Dream Imagery: Relationship to rapid eye movements of sleep. *Archives of General Psychiatry, 152*, p. 239.

11. Herman, J. H., Erman, M., Boys, R., Peiser, L., Taylor, M. E. and Roffwarg, H. P. (1984) Evidence for a directional correspondence between eye movements and dream imagery in REM sleep. *Sleep, 7*, 52–63.

12. Amadeo, M. and Gomez, E. (1966) Eye movements, attention and dreaming in subjects with lifelong blindness. *Canadian Psychiatric Association Journal, 11*, 500–507. See also Gross, J., Byrne, J. and Fisher, C. (1965) Eye movements during emergent Stage I EEG in subjects with life-long blindness. *Journal of Nervous and Mental Disease, 141*, 365–370.

13. Jacobs, L., Feldman, M. and Bender, M. B. (1972) Are the eye movements of dreaming sleep related to the visual images of dreams? *Psychophysiology, 20*, 393–401.

14. Fisher, C. (1966) Dreaming and sexuality. *Psychoanalysis-A General Psychology*, 537–569.

15. Hauri, P. and Van de Castle, R. L. (1973) Psychophysiological parallels in dreams. *Psychosomatic Medicine, 35*, 297–308.

16. Hobson, J. A., Goldfrank, F. and Snyder, F. (1965) Respiration and mental activity in sleep. *Journal of Psychiatric Research, 3*, 79–90.

17. Ibid. p. 86.

18. Goodenough, D. R., Witkin, H. A., Koulack, D. and Cohen, H. (1975) The effects of stress films on dream affect and on respiration and eye-movement activity during rapid-eye-movement sleep. *Psychophysiology, 12*, 313–320.

19. Koulack, D. (1972) Rapid eye movements and visual imagery during sleep. *Psychological Bulletin, 78*, 155–158.

20. Luborsky, L., Blinder, B. and Mackworth, N. (1963) Eye fixation and recall of pictures as a function of GSR responsiv-

ity. *Perceptual and Motor Skills, 16* (Monograph Suppl. No. 5), 469–483.

21. Goodenough, Witkin, Koulack and Cohen, The effects of stress films on dream affect and on respiration and eye-movement activity during rapid-eye-movement sleep.

22. Hauri and Van de Castle, Psychophysiological parallels in dreams.

Chapter 5. Daytime Events, Sleep and Dreaming

1. Agnew, H. W., Webb, W. B. and Williams, R. L. (1966) The first night effect: An EEG study of sleep. *Psychophysiology, 2,* 263–266. And Webb, W. B. and Campbell, S. S. (1979) The first night effect revisited with age as a variable. *Waking Sleep, 3,* 319–324.

2. Dement, W. C., Kahn, E. and Roffwarg, H. P. (1965) The influence of the laboratory situation on the dreams of the experimental subject. *The Journal of Nervous and Mental Disease, 140,* 119–131. And Hall, C. S. (1967) Representation of the laboratory setting in dreams. *The Journal of Nervous and Mental Disease, 144,* 198–206.

3. Coble, P., McPartland, R. J., Silva, W. J. and Kupfer, D. J. (1974) Is there a first night effect? (a revisit) *Biological Psychiatry, 9,* 215–219. And Browman, C. P. and Cartwright, R. D. (1980) The first-night effect on sleep and dreams. *Biological Psychiatry, 15,* 809–812.

4. Witkin, H. A. and Lewis, H. B. (1967) Presleep experiences and dreams. In H. A. Witkin and H. B. Lewis (Eds.) *Experimental studies of dreaming.* New York: Random House, pp. 164–165.

5. Ibid., p. 166.

6. Witkin, H. A. (1969) Influencing dream content. In M. Kramer (Ed.) *Dream psychology and the new biology of dreaming.* Springfield: Charles C. Thomas, p. 318.

7. Ibid., p. 319.

8. Goodenough, D. R., Witkin, H. A., Koulack, D. and Cohen, H. (1975) The effects of stress films on dream affect and on

respiration and eye-movement activity during rapid-eye-movement sleep. *Psychophysiology, 12,* 313–320.

9. Collins, G., Davison, L. A., and Breger, L. (1967) Dream function in adaptation to threat: A preliminary study. Paper read at the 7th annual meeting of the Association for the Psychophysiological Study of Sleep, Santa Monica, California.

10. Cartwright, R. D., Kasniak, A., Borowitz, G., and Kling, A. (1972) The dreams of homosexual and heterosexual subjects to the same erotic movie. *Psychophysiology, 9,* 117.

11. Baekeland, F., Koulack, D. and Lasky, R. (1968) Effects of a stressful presleep experience on electroencephalograph-recorded sleep. *Psychophysiology, 4,* 436–443.

12. Koulack, D., Prevost, F. and De Koninck, J. (1985) Sleep, dreaming, and adaptation to a stressful intellectual activity. *Sleep, 8,* 244–253.

13. Wright, J. S. and Koulack, D. (1988) Dreams and adaptation to a stressful intellectual activity. Poster presented at the conference on Sleep and the Quality of Waking Life at Winnipeg, Manitoba.

14. Breger, L., Hunter, I. and Lane, R. W. (1971) The effects of stress on dreams. *Psychological Issues, 7* (3, Monograph 27).

15. Melstrom, M. A. and Cartwright, R. D. (1983) Effects of successful vs. unsuccessful psychotherapy outcome on some dream dimensions. *Psychiatry, 46,* 51–65.

16. Koulack, D., LeBow, M. D. and Church, M. (1976) The effect of desensitization on the sleep and dreams of a phobic subject. *Canadian Journal of Behavioural Science, 8,* 418–421.

17. Bergin, A. E. (1970) A note on dream change following desensitization. *Behavior Therapy, 1,* 546–549.

18. Theroux, C. (1979) *The adaptive function of dreams in dealing with stress.* Unpublished Doctoral Dissertation, University of Manitoba.

19. Ullman, M. (1987) Dreams and society. In M. Ullman and C. Limmer (Eds.) *The variety of dream experience: Expanding our ways of working with dreams.* New York: Continuum.

20. Rados, R. and Cartwright, R. D. (1982) Where do dreams come from? A comparison of presleep and REM sleep thematic content. *Journal of Abnormal Psychology, 91,* 433–436.

21. Witkin and Lewis, Presleep experiences and dreams. And Bertini, M., Lewis, H. B. and Witkin, H. A. (1964) Some preliminary observations with an experimental procedure from the study of hypnagogic and related phenomena. *Archivo di Psicologia Neurologia e Psychiatria, 6,* 493–534. (Also printed in a condensed form in C. T. Tart [Ed.] [1969] *Altered states of consciousness.* New York: Wiley.)

22. Vogel, G., Foulkes, D., and Trosman, H. (1966) Ego functions and dreaming during sleep onset. *Archives of General Psychiatry, 14,* 238–248.

23. Hall, C. S. (1984) A "ubiquitous sex difference in dreams" revisited. *Journal of Personality and Social Psychology, 46,* 1109–1117.

24. Lortie-Lussier, M., Schwab, C. and De Koninck, J. (1985) Working mothers versus homemakers: Do dreams reflect the changing roles of women? *Sex roles, 12,* 1009–1021.

25. Kramer, M., Kinney, L. and Scharf, M. (1983) Sex differences in dreams. *The Psychiatric Journal of the University of Ottawa, 8,* 1–4.

26. Foulkes, D. (1981) *Children's dreams.* New York: Wiley.

27. Blick, K. A. and Howe, J. B. (1984) A comparison of the emotional content of dreams recalled by young and elderly women. *The Journal of Psychology, 116,* 143–146.

28. Piccione, P., Jacobs, G., Kramer, M. and Roth, T. (1977) The relationship between daily activities, emotions and dream content. *Sleep Research, 6,* 133.

29. Koulack, D. (1986) Effects of presleep and during-sleep stimuli on the content of dreams. In J. Gackenbach (Ed.) *Sleep and dreams: A sourcebook.* New York: Garland Publishing, Inc., p. 214.

30. Ibid., p. 215.

31. Bagby, E. (1930) Dreams during periods of emotional stress. *Journal of Abnormal and Social Psychology, 25,* 289–292.

32. Cartwright, R. D., Lloyd, S., Knight, S. and Trenholme, I. (1984) Broken dreams: A study of the effects of divorce and depression on dream content. *Psychiatry, 47,* 251–259.

33. Aron, A. (1988) The collective nightmare of Salvadoran refugees. Paper presented at the Fifth International Conference of the Association for the Study of Dreams, Santa Cruz, California.

34. Wilmar, H. A. (1982) Vietnam and madness: Dreams of schizophrenic veterans. *The Journal of the American Academy of Psychoanalysis, 10,* 47–65.

35. Starker, S. and Jolin, A. (1982–83) Imagery and fantasy in Vietnam veteran psychiatric inpatients. *Imagination, Cognition and Personality, 2,* 15–22.

36. Kramer, M. and Kinney, L. (1988) Sleep patterns in trauma victims. *Psychiatric Journal of the University of Ottawa, 13,* 12–16.

Chapter 6. Our Bodies, Our Dreams

1. Koulack, D., De Koninck, J., and Oczkowski, G. (1978) Field dependence and the effect of REM deprivation on thirst. *Perceptual and Motor Skills, 46,* 559–562.

2. Bokert, E. (1967) *The effects of thirst and a related auditory stimulus on dream reports.* Unpublished Doctoral Dissertation, New York University.

3. Koulack, D. (1970) Effects of thirst on the sleep cycle. *The Journal of Nervous and Mental Disease, 151,* 143–145.

4. Browman, C. P. (1980) Sleep following sustained physical exercise. *Psychophysiology, 17,* 577–580.

5. Bunnell, D. E., Bevier, W. C. and Horvath, S. M. (1983) Nocturnal sleep, cardiovascular function, and adrenal activity following maximum-capacity exercise. *Electroencephalography and Clinical Neurophysiology, 56,* 186–189.

6. Torsvall, L. and Akerstedt, T. (1983) Different degrees of physical exertion: Their effects on sleep. In W. P. Koella (Ed.) *Sleep 1982.*

7. Hauri, P. (1969) The influence of evening activity on the onset of sleep. *Psychophysiology, 5,* 426–430.

8. Hauri, P. (1970) Evening activity, sleep mentation, and subjective sleep quality. *Journal of Abnormal Psychology, 76,* 270–275.

9. Ibid.

10. Carroll, D., Lewis, S. A. and Oswald, I. (1969) Effect of barbiturates on dream content. *Nature, 223,* 865–866.

11. Kales, A., Malstrom, E. J., Kee, H. K., Kales, J. D. and Tan, T.-L. (1969) Effects of hypnotics on sleep patterns, dreaming, and mood state: Laboratory and home studies. *Biological Psychiatry, 1,* 235–241.

12. Gross, M. M., Goodenough, D., Tobin, M., Halpert, E., Lepore, D., Perlstein, A., Sirota, M., Dibianco, J., Fuller, R. and Kishner, I. (1966) Sleep disturbances and hallucinations in the acute alcohol psychosis. *The Journal of Nervous and Mental Disease, 142,* 493–514.

13. MacLean, A. W. and Cairns, J. (1982) Dose response of ethanol on the sleep of young men. *Journal of Studies on Alcohol, 43,* 434–444.

14. Gresham, S. C., Webb, W. B., Williams, R. L. (1963) Alcohol and caffeine: Effect on inferred visual dreaming. *Science, 140,* 1226–1227.

15. Greenberg, R. and Pearlman, C. (1967) Delirium tremens and dreaming. *The American Journal of Psychiatry, 124,* 37–46.

16. Wolin, S. J. and Mello, N. K. (1973) The effects of alcohol on dreams and hallucinations in alcohol addicts. *Annals of the New York Academy of Sciences, 215,* 266–302.

17. Zimmerman, E. and Parlee, M. B. (1973) Behavioral changes associated with the menstrual cycle: An experimental investigation. *Journal of Applied Social Psychology, 3,* 335–344.

18. Dalton, K. (1979) *The menstrual cycle.* London: Penguin Books.

19. Hartmann, E. (1966) Dreaming sleep (the D-state) and the menstrual cycle. *The Journal of Nervous and Mental Disease, 143,* 406–416.

20. Ho, M. A. (1972) *Sex hormones and the sleep of women.* Unpublished Doctoral Dissertation, Yeshiva University.

21. Garfield, P. L. (1974) Women, blood and dreams. *Sleep Research, 3,* 106.

22. Trinder, J., Van de Castle, R., Bourne, R. and Frisbie, D. (1973) Dream recall as a function of the menstrual cycle. *Sleep Research, 2,* 114.

23. Schultz, K. J. and Koulack, D. (1980) Dream affect and the menstrual cycle. *The Journal of Nervous and Mental Disease, 168,* 436–438.

24. Sirois-Berliss, M. and De Koninck, J. (1982) Menstrual stress and dreams: Adaptation or interference? *The Psychiatric Journal of the University of Ottawa, 7,* 77–86.

25. Breger, L., Hunter, I. and Lane, R. W. (1971) The effects of stress on dreams. *Psychological Issues, 7* (3, Monograph 27).

26. Sharpe, E. F. (1959) *Dream analysis.* London: The Hogarth Press.

27. Smith, R. C. (1984) A possible biologic role of dreaming. *Psychotherapy and Psychosomatics, 41,* 167–176.

28. Smith, R. C. (1987) Do dreams reflect a biological state? *The Journal of Nervous and Mental Disease, 175,* 201–207.

29. Armstrong, R., Burnap, D., Jacobson, A., Kales, A., Ward, S., and Golden, J. (1965) Dreams and gastric secretion in duodenal ulcer patients. *New Physician, 14,* 241–243.

30. Hartmann, E. (1966) The D-state (dreaming sleep) and psychosomatic illness. *Psychosomatic Medicine, 134,* 203–206.

31. Levitan, H. (1983) Dreams which precipitate asthma attacks. In A. J. Krakowski and C. P. Kimball (Eds.) *Psychosomatic Medicine: Theoretical, clinical and transcultural aspects.* New York: Plenum.

32. Foy, A. L. (1970) Dreams of patients and staff. *American Journal of Nursing, 70,* 80–82.

Chapter 7. Things That Go Bump in the Night

1. Freud, S. (1965) *The interpretation of dreams.* (J. Strachey, trans.) New York: Avon, pp. 61–62. (Originally published, 1900.)

2. Maury, L. F. A. (1861) *Le sommeil et les rêves.* Paris: Didier and Co.

3. Cubberly, A. J. (1923) The effects of tensions of the body surface upon the normal dream. *British Journal of Psychology, 13,* 243–265.

4. Dement, W. C. and Wolpert, E. A. (1958) The relation of eye movements, body motility, and external stimuli to dream content. *Journal of Experimental Psychology, 55,* 543–553.

5. Berger, R. J. (1963) Experimental modification of dream content by meaningful verbal stimuli. *The British Journal of Psychiatry, 109,* 722–740.

6. Koulack, D. (1969) Effects of somatosensory stimulation on dream content. *Archives of General Psychiatry, 20,* 718–725.

7. Ibid., p. 721.

8. Freud, *The interpretation of dreams,* p. 267.

9. Burton, S. A., Harsh, J. R. and Badia, P. (1988) Cognitive activity in sleep and responsiveness to external stimuli. *Sleep, 11,* 61–68.

10. Hoelscher, T. J., Klinger, E. and Barta, S. G. (1981) Incorporation of concern- and nonconcern-related verbal stimuli into dream content. *Journal of Abnormal Psychology, 90,* 88–91.

11. De Koninck, J.-M. and Koulack, D. (1975) Dream content and adaptation to a stressful situation. *Journal of Abnormal Psychology, 84,* 250–260.

12. Koulack, D. (1986) Effects of presleep and during-sleep stimuli on the content of dreams. In J. Gackenbach (Ed.) *Sleep and dreams: A sourcebook.* New York: Garland Publishing, Inc., p. 219.

13. Evans, F. J., Gustafson, L. A., O'Connell, D. N., Orne, M. T. and Shor, R. E. (1970) Verbally induced behavioral responses during sleep. *The Journal of Nervous and Mental Disease, 150,* 171–187.

14. Perry, C. W., Evans, F. J., O'Connell, D. N., Orne, E. C. and Orne, M. T. (1978) Behavioral response to verbal stimuli administered and tested during REM sleep: A further investigation. *Waking and Sleeping, 2,* 35–42.

15. Wilson, W. P. and Zung, W. W. K. (1966) Attention, discrimination and arousal during sleep. *Archives of General Psychiatry, 15,* 523–528.

16. Bertini, M., Gregolini, H. and Vitali, S. (1971) Dream research: A new experimental approach. Paper presented at the 11th annual meeting of the Association for the Psychophysiological Study of Sleep, Bruges, Belgium.

17. Emmons, W. H. and Simon, C. W. (1956) The nonrecall of material presented during sleep. *American Journal of Psychology, 69,* 76–81. And Simon, C. W. and Emmons, W. H. (1956) Responses to material presented during various levels of sleep. *Journal of Experimental Psychology, 51,* 89–97.

18. Bruce, D. J., Evans, C. R., Fenwick, P. B. C. and Spencer, V. (1970) Effect of presenting novel verbal material during slow-wave sleep. *Nature, 225,* 873–874.

Chapter 8. Dream Recall and Dream Recall Failure

1. Freud, S. (1965) *The interpretation of dreams.* (J. Strachey, trans.) New York: Avon, pp. 555–556. (Originally published, 1900.)

2. Ibid., p. 559.

3. Webb, W. B. and Kersey, J. (1967) Recall of dreams and the probability of stage 1-REM sleep. *Perceptual and Motor Skills, 24,* 627–630.

4. Wolpert, E. A. (1972) Two classes of factors affecting dream recall. *Journal of the American Psychoanalytic Association, 20,* 45–58.

5. Whitman, R., Kramer, M. and Baldridge, B. (1963) Which dream does the patient tell? *Archives of General Psychiatry, 8,* 277–282.

6. Weisz, R. and Foulkes, D. (1970) Home and laboratory dreams collected under uniform sampling conditions. *Psychophysiology, 6,* 588–596.

7. Goodenough, D. R. (1967) Some recent studies of dream recall. In H. A. Witkin and H. B. Lewis (Eds.) *Experimental studies of dreaming.* New York: Random House.

8. Koulack, D. (1970) Repression and forgetting of dreams. In M. Bertini (Ed.) *Psicofisiologia del sonno e del sogno.* Milano: Editrice Vita e Pensiero.

9. Cohen, D. B. (1972) Presleep experience and home dream reporting: An exploratory study. *Journal of Consulting and Clinical Psychology, 38,* 122–128.

10. Holmes, M. (1973) *REM sleep patterning and dream recall in convergers and divergers: Evidence for different defensive preferences.* Occasional paper No. 16 of the Centre for Research in the Educational Sciences, University of Edinburgh.

11. Goodenough, D. R., Witkin, H. A., Lewis, H. B., Koulack, D., and Cohen, H. (1974) Repression, interference and field dependence as factors in dream forgetting. *Journal of Abnormal Psychology, 83,* 32–44.

12. Cohen, D. B. (1974) Toward a theory of dream recall. *Psychological Bulletin, 81,* 138–154.

13. Cohen, D. B. and Wolfe, G. (1973) Dream recall and repression: Evidence for an alternative hypothesis. *Journal of Consulting and Clinical Psychology, 41,* 349–355.

14. Goodenough, D. R., Shapiro, A., Holden, M. and Steinschriber, L. A. (1959) A comparison of "dreamers" and "nondreamers": Eye movements, electroencephalograms, and the recall of dreams. *The Journal of Abnormal and Social Psychology, 59*, 295–302.

15. Barber, B. (1969) *Factors underlying individual differences in rate of dream reporting.* Unpublished Doctoral Dissertation, Yeshiva University.

16. Trinder, J. and Kramer, M. (1971) Dream recall. *American Journal of Psychiatry, 128*, 296–301.

17. Ibid.

18. Meier, C. A., Ruef, H., Ziegler, A. and Hall, C. S. (1968) Forgetting of dreams in the laboratory. *Perceptual and Motor Skills, 26*, 551–557.

19. Shapiro, A., Goodenough, D. R., and Gryler, R. B. (1963) Dream recall as a function of the method of awakening. *Psychosomatic Medicine, 25*, 174–180.

20. Rechtschaffen, A., Hauri, P. and Zeitlan, M. (1966) Auditory awakening thresholds in REM and NREM sleep stages. *Perceptual and Motor Skills, 22*, 927–942.

21. Jus, K., Kiljan, A., Kubacki, A., Losieczko, T., Wilczak, H. and Jus, A. (1969) Experimental studies on memory during slow sleep stages and REM stages. *Electroencephalography and Clinical Neurophysiology, 27*, 668.

22. Goodenough, D. R., Sapan, J., Cohen, H., Portnoff, G. and Shapiro, A. (1971) Some experiments concerning the effects of sleep on memory. *Psychophysiology, 8*, 749–762.

23. Koulack, D. and Goodenough, D. R. (1976) Dream recall and dream recall failure: An arousal-retrieval model. *Psychological Bulletin, 83*, 975–984. See also Koulack, D. and Goodenough, D. R. (1977) Modèle de rappel des rêves au réveil, proposé pour rendre compte des défauts de souvenirs des rêves. *Annales Médico-Psychologiques, 135*, 35–42.

24. Cory, T., Ormiston, D. W., Simmel, E. and Dainoff, M. (1975) Predicting the frequency of dream recall. *Journal of Abnormal Psychology, 84*, 261–266.

25. Koulack, D. (1975) Dream affect and dream recall. In P. Levin and W. P. Koella (Eds.) *Sleep 1974*. Basel, Switzerland: Karger.

26. De Koninck, J. -M. and Koulack, D. (1975) Dream content and adaptation to a stressful situation. *Journal of Abnormal Psychology, 84*, 250–260.

Chapter 9. Dream Deprivation

1. Freud, S. (1965) *The interpretation of dreams*. (J. Strachey, trans.) New York: Avon, p. 115. (Originally published, 1900.)

2. Ibid., p. 115.

3. Ibid., p. 647.

4. Gross, M. M., Goodenough, D., Tobin, M., Halpert, E., Lepore, D., Pearlstein, A., Sirota, M., Dibianco, J., Fuller, R. and Kishner, I. (1966) Sleep disturbances and hallucinations in the acute alcohol psychosis. *The Journal of Nervous and Mental Disease, 142*, 493–514. And Greenberg, R. and Pearlman, C. (1967) Delirium tremens and dreaming. *American Journal of Psychiatry, 124*, 133–142.

5. Kales, A., Hoedemaker, F., Jacobson, A. and Lichtenstein, E. (1964) Dream deprivation: An experimental reappraisal. *Nature, 204*, 1337–1338.

6. Dement W. and Fisher, C. (1963) Experimental interference with the sleep cycle. *Canadian Psychiatric Association Journal, 8*, 400–405.

7. Sampson, H. (1966) Psychological effects of deprivation of dreaming sleep. *Journal of Nervous and Mental Disease, 143*, 305–317.

8. Dement, W. (1960) The effect of dream deprivation. *Science, 131*, 1705.

9. Agnew, H. W. Jr., Webb, W. B. and Williams, R. L. (1967) Comparison of stage four and 1-REM sleep deprivation. *Perceptual and Motor Skills, 24*, 851–858.

10. Ferguson, J. and Dement, W. (1965) REM sleep in cats on varied sleep-wakefulness schedules. Paper presented at the 5th annual meeting of the Association for the Psychophysiological Study of Sleep, Washington, D.C.

11. Dement, W., Greenberg, A. and Klein, R. (1965) The persistence of the REM deprivation effect. Paper presented at the 5th annual meeting of the Association for the Psychophysiological Study of Sleep, Washington, D. C.

12. Salamy, J. (1971) Effects of REM deprivation and awakening on instrumental performance during stage 2 and REM sleep. *Biological Psychiatry, 3*, 321–330.

13. Webb, W. and Agnew, H. (1965) Sleep: The effects of a restricted regime. *Science, 150*, 1745–1747.

14. Kales, A., Tan, T.-L., Kollar, E. J., Naitoh, P., Preston, T. A., and Malstrom, E. J. (1970) Sleep patterns following 205 hours of sleep deprivation. *Psychosomatic Medicine, 32*, 189–200.

15. Roffwarg, H. P., Muzio, J. and Dement, W. C. (1966) Ontogenetic development of the human sleep-dream cycle. *Science, 152*, 604–619.

16. Ephron, H. S. and Carrington, P. (1966) Rapid eye movement sleep and cortical homeostasis. *Psychological Review, 73*, 500–526.

17. Snyder, F. (1966) Toward an evolutionary theory of dreaming. *American Journal of Psychiatry, 2*, 121–136.

18. Hobson, J. A. and McCarley, R. W. (1977) The brain as a dream state generator: An activation-synthesis hypothesis of the dream process. *American Journal of Psychiatry, 134*, 1335–1348.

19. Horne, J. (1988) *Why we sleep. The functions of sleep in humans and other mammals.* Oxford University Press: Oxford, England.

20. Ibid., p. 305.

21. Dement, W. C. (1978) *Some must watch while some must sleep.* W. W. Norton & Company, Inc.: New York.

22. Halper, C., Pivik, T. and Dement, W. (1969) An attempt to reduce the REM rebound following REM deprivation by the use of waking mentation. Paper presented at a meeting of the Association for the Psychophysiological Study of Sleep, Boston, Massachusetts.

23. Tart, C. T. (1964) A comparison of suggested dreams occurring in hypnosis and sleep. *International Journal of Clinical and Experimental Hypnosis, 12*, 263–289.

24. Cartwright, R. D., Monroe, L. J. and Palmer, C. (1967) Individual differences in response to REM deprivation. *Archives of General Psychiatry, 16*, 297–303.

25. Cartwright, R. D. and Monroe, L. J. (1968) Relation of dreaming and REM sleep: The effects of REM deprivation under two conditions. *Journal of Personality and Social Psychology, 10*, 69–74.

26. Koulack, D. (1973) Effects of a hypnagogic type situation and a dull task on subsequent REM-rebound: A preliminary report. In M. H. Chase, W. C. Stern, and P. L. Walter (Eds.) *Sleep Research, 2*. Los Angeles, California: Brain Information Service/Brain Research Institute, University of California, p. 167.

27. Dinges, D. (1989) Imagery during hypnopompic states. Paper presented at the Arizona Conference on Sleep and Cognition, Tucson, Arizona.

Chapter 10. The Adaptive Function of Dreams

1. Freud, S. (1965) *The interpretation of dreams.* (J. Strachey, trans.) New York: Avon. (Originally published, 1900).

2. Dallett, J. (1973) Theories of dream function. *Psychological Bulletin, 79*, 408–416.

3. Breger, L. (1967) Function of Dreams. *Journal of Abnormal Psychology, 72*, (Monograph No. 5, Whole No. 641), 1–28.

4. Ibid., p. 27.

5. Ibid.

6. Cohen, D. B. and Cox, C. (1975) Neuroticism in the sleep laboratory: Implications for representational and adaptive properties of dreaming. *Journal of Abnormal Psychology, 84,* 91–108.

7. Koulack, D., Prevost, F. and De Koninck, J. (1985) Sleep, dreaming, and adaptation to a stressful intellectual activity. *Sleep, 8,* 244–253.

8. Greenberg, R., Pearlman, C., Brooks, R., Mayer, R. and Hartmann, E. (1968) Dreaming and Korsakoff's psychosis. *Archives of General Psychiatry, 18,* 203–208.

9. Koulack, D. and Goodenough, D. R. (1976) Dream recall and dream recall failure: An arousal-retrieval model. *Psychological Bulletin, 83,* 975–984. And Koulack, D. and Goodenough, D. R. (1977) Modèle de rappel des rêves au réveil, proposé pour rendre compte des défauts de souvenirs des rêves. *Annales Médico-Psychologiques, 135,* 35–42.

10. Greenberg, R., Pearlman, C., Fingar, R., Kantrowitz, J. and Kawliche, S. (1970) The effects of dream deprivation: Implications for a theory of the psychological function of dreaming. *British Journal of Medical Psychology, 43,* 1–11.

11. Ibid., p. 9.

12. Greiser, C., Greenberg, R. and Harrison, R. H. (1972) The adaptive function of sleep: The differential effects of sleep and dreaming on recall. *Journal of Abnormal Psychology, 80,* 280–286.

13. Ibid., p. 285.

14. Greenberg, R., Pillard, R. and Pearlman, C. (1972) The effect of dream deprivation on adaptation to stress. *Psychosomatic Medicine, 34,* 257–262.

15. De Koninck, J. -M. and Koulack, D. (1975) Dream content and adaptation to a stressful situation. *Journal of Abnormal Psychology, 84,* 250–260.

16. Jung, C. G. (1956) *Two essays on analytical psychology.* New York: Meridian Books.

212 *To Catch A Dream*

17. Ibid., p. 186.

18. Jung, C. G. (1933) *Modern man in search of a soul.* New York: Harcourt, Brace & World, Inc., p. 17.

19. Wood, P. (1962) *Dreaming and social isolation.* Unpublished Doctoral Dissertation, University of North Carolina.

20. Hauri, P. (1970) Evening activity, sleep mentation, and subjective quality of sleep. *Journal of Abnormal Psychology, 76,* 270–275.

21. Foulkes, D., Pivik, T., Steadman, H. S., Spear, P. S. and Symonds, J. D. (1967) Dreams of the male child: An EEG study. *Journal of Abnormal Psychology, 72,* 457–467.

22. Koulack, D. (1987) Dreams and adaptation to contemporary stress. Paper presented at a symposium on Dreams at the 5th International Congress of Sleep Research, Copenhagen, Denmark.

23. Koulack, D., LeBow, M. D. and Church, M. (1976) The effect of desensitization on the sleep and dreams of a phobic subject. *Canadian Journal of Behavioural Science, 8,* 418–421.

24. Kramer, M. and Roth, T. (1973) The mood-regulating function of sleep. In W. P. Koella and P. Levin (Eds.) *Sleep: Physiology, biochemistry, psychology, pharmacology, clinical implications.* Basel: Karger. And Kramer, M. (1987) The mood regulatory function of dreaming: The dream as selective affective modulator. Paper presented at a symposium on Dreams at the 5th International Congress of Sleep Research, Copenhagen, Denmark.

25. Wright, J. and Koulack, D. (1987) Dreams and contemporary stress: A disruption-avoidance-adaptation model. *Sleep, 10,* 172–179.

26. Ibid.

27. Lauer, C., Riemann, R., Lund, R. and Berger, M. (1987) Shortened REM latency: A consequence of psychological strain. *Psychophysiology, 24,* 263–271.

28. Ibid., p. 269.

29. Wright, J. S. and Koulack, D. (1988) Dreams and adaptation to a stressful intellectual activity. Poster presented at the conference on Sleep and the Quality of Waking Life at Winnipeg, Manitoba.

INDEX